D0909945

The Man Whom Women Loved

THE MAN WHOM WOMEN LOVED

The Life of Bror Blixen

ULF ASCHAN

ST. MARTIN'S PRESS

New York

Design by Claire B. Counihan

Library of Congress Cataloging-in-Publication Data

Aschan, Ulf.
The man whom women loved.

1. Dinesen, Isak, 1885–1962. 2. Authors, Danish—20th century—Biography. 3. Blixen-Finecke, Bror, baron von, 1886–1946. 4. Hunters—Kenya—Biography. 5. Husbands—Kenya—Biography. 6. Kenya—Social Life and customs. I. Title.
PT8175.B545Z57 1987 839.8'1372 [B] 87-16508
ISBN 0-312-00064-2

First published in Sweden by Förlags AB Wiken under the title *Baron Blixen: Ett Porträtt av Baron Bror von Blixen-Finecke.*

First U.S. Edition

10 9 8 7 6 5 4 3 2 1

CONTENTS

ACKNOWLEDGMENTS

CAN NEVER ADEQUATELY CONVEY my immense appreciation and sincere thanks to the following, without whom there would never have been a book: Krister Aschan, my father, in loving memory, for all his photographs and his memoir on Blix; Marianne, my life companion, whose positive criticism, encouragement, and support has been of tremendous value; Romolus Kleen, whose notes and research are the backbone of the book; Sarah Seth-Smith, whose patience by the typewriter, endless corrections, and invaluable advice cannot be measured; Claes and Tony Lewenhaupt, whose tireless and professional assistance with all the photographs was remarkable; Judith Thurman, whose idea it was; and Christer Strandberg.

If I were to express the proper gratitude I feel to all those others who have encouraged me, helped me, talked to me, lent me their precious photographs, offered me hospitality, read my manuscript, and pushed me, it would become a book on its own. Please accept that I only list your names.

Kristina Anjou; Anne Bjerke; Dick von Blixen Finecke; Hans von Blixen Finecke; Doria Block; Rose Cartwright; Arthur and Tobina Cole; Olle Dickson; Ingeborg Dinesen; Polly Peabody Drysdale; Kristina Fallenius; Ette Fjastad; Elisabeth and Jan Gregory; Carin von Haffner; Roul Hamilton, Sr.; Ebba Hamilton; Lillian Herslow; Marian Hobson; Anders Holmberg; Andrew Holmberg; Cockie Hoogterp; Adrian House; Elspeth Huxley; John King; Ake Lindstrom; Manon

Lovelace; Mary Lovell; Diana Guest Manning; Beryl Markham; Charles Markham; Gustaf Martin; Henry de Montesquieu; Christopher Munika; Gerald Nevill; Wilhelm Penser; Fredrik af Petersens; Dorothy Percival; Joan Peters; Ruth Rasmusson; Gerald Rilling; Ulric von Rosen; Carl Rosenorn-Lehn; Fritz Rosenorn-Lehn; Otto Rosenorn-Lehn; Mauro Saio; Pamela Scott; Shreekesh Shah; Candy Seymour-Smith; Lene Silfverschiold; Viweka Stiernsward; Brian Stutchbury; Dorothea Tham; Sebastian Tham; Simon Trevor; Gustaf Trolle-Bonde; Brita Vanneck; Anne Winston.

Blickie's wife (Isak Dinesen) is a damn sight better writer than any Swede they ever gave it (the Nobel prize) to and Blickie is in hell and he would be pleased if I spoke well of his wife.

—ERNEST HEMINGWAY

INTRODUCTION

URING WORLD WAR II, my parents lived in Stockholm. From time to time, wild laughter and animation were inspired by the presence of a visitor, a radiant, sunburned extrovert. To me, a little boy listening, he was pure magic. This was Baron Blixen, my godfather. My fascination with him never ceased. His visits conjured up a longing to be a part of the mystery he brought out of Africa—adventure, wild country, exotic animals, and unknown people.

The Blixen name has lived on through the elegant and poetic writings of his wife, Karen, who captured the admiration of lovers of the English language, especially in America, where her book *Out of Africa* eventually appeared in English literature courses. Critical books on her work and life proliferated. A personality cult grew.

Meryl Streep's interpretation of Karen Blixen in the film *Out of Africa* was a culmination of everything anyone had been able to imagine about Karen Blixen: the great charmer with beguiling ways, courage, and love of beauty. With this heightened personality cult, Blix, by inference, was relegated to a most unsympathetic role. The balance was strained—her qualities were exalted and his discounted. In some way the balance should be adjusted. This is why I am writing this book.

Blix was a man larger than life. Spending freely, he took

what life had to offer and went where adventure beckoned. Failure and sorrow were laughed aside, metamorphosed by new and changing experiences. Neither counting the cost nor weighing the consequences, he lived to enjoy the minute.

Ulf Aschan
Nairobi, 1986

The Man Whom Women Loved

Hunting with Blix was a magnificent experience. With his quiet, almost lyrical narrative of what happened around us, he got nature to live like I have never experienced since.

—EBBA HAMILTON

One

Family, Childhood, and Youth: 1886–1912

LIX'S GRANDFATHER, Carl Frederik, was born in 1822 and became Minister for Foreign Affairs in Denmark at the age of thirty-seven. He, like Blix, had a keen eye for pretty women. This landed Carl Frederik in trouble at a royal dinner in 1854 when he paid too much attention to the queen's sister, Princess Augusta of Hessen. The pair had quietly withdrawn and closeted themselves in an anteroom for a tête-à-tête when they were discovered by his wife. Incensed, she locked the door in protest. The incident created such a scandal that his wife was expected to divorce him, and eventually did. Carl Frederik married the Princess.

Soon the whole of European aristocracy revolved around the new couple. At a royal shoot at Nasbyholm, the Blixen family estate in Sweden, King Charles XV, Crown Prince Oscar, the Prince of Hessen, Prince Otto von Bismarck, and the Austrian Baron d'Oriola were among the guests.

In the warm weather, the veranda doors at Nasbyholm were left open, giving the onlookers a spectacular view of the evening's entertainment. On one occasion, a knot of commoners had gathered outside, hoping to catch a glimpse of the king himself, who many expected would be wearing a crown. The king spotted a young girl in the crowd and declared her "the prettiest girl in all the country." He expressed a wish to join her outside, but he was prevented from this sudden breach of protocol by his aide de camp. He then had to content himself with offering her delicacies through the open window. She blushingly accepted, to the resounding cheers of the crowd.

Carl Frederik and Princess Augusta had two sons, Frederik and Gustaf. Gustaf, the younger, joined the Swedish Cavalry and became aide de camp to Crown Prince Gustaf, later King Gustaf V of Sweden. The Crown Prince and his wife, Victoria, planned to spend the winter of 1890–1891 in Egypt, as the climate was thought good for her delicate constitution. Gustaf von Blixen went with them.

The Crown Princess and Blixen discovered that they shared the same interest in photography. He became her constant companion, assisting in the developing and processing, which took place in a special tent erected in the desert as a darkroom. Whether there was an attempt to develop a more intimate relationship can only be surmised from a letter written to King Oscar by a friend: "The relationship between the two [Victoria and the Crown Prince] has become somewhat chilly, but the splendid and delightful Baron Gustaf von Blixen has undoubtedly made a certain impression on her." The Crown Prince agreed that Blixen should not accompany them on the next trip to Egypt, "so that people will not have cause to gossip."

This dashing young officer never married. His elder brother, Frederik, inherited Nasbyholm.

Frederik married Clara Krag-Juel-Vind-Frijs, and they became the parents of seven children, including Blix. They were a remarkable and well-loved couple, and Frederik was always referred to as "the gentle Baron." Clara was very social

Gustaf von Blixen, right, was considered one of the most charming and attractive bachelors of his time. He made a strong impression on Crown Princess Victoria and their romance during the Egypt trip was openly talked about.

Crown Prince Gustaf is holding the binoculars; the party was photographed outside Cairo.

6

and loved house parties and entertaining, which the retiring Baron sometimes found disturbed his need for more quiet pursuits. It was his shy, retiring nature that caused him to turn down important positions within the country. He was reluctant to be seen in public. When his cattle won prizes at shows, he delegated to his steward the honor of accepting the prizes. He was an excellent horseman and outstanding shot; his shoots were famous, and an invitation to shoot at Nasbyholm was highly sought after.

Frederik and Clara had three sons and four daughters. Blix and his twin brother, Hans, were the youngest. The twins were extremely close. Theirs was a happy childhood. They shared a deep love for the country and the outdoors. They wandered unchecked through Nasbyholm's forests and grounds,which abounded with game birds, deer, hare, and rabbit. Gamekeepers tended to turn a blind eye to the boys poaching the odd rabbit or two. No harm was done, and besides, it kept the boys out of other trouble and in pocket money (selling to the local butcher). Observing life's natural pattern at close range instilled in them deep-seated feelings of independence and a mastery of their own fate.

It was therefore with scant enthusiasm that the twins eventually left this idyllic life to take their first steps into the world of academe. In Blix's case, these steps were not always sure-footed. Outside the classroom, Hans and Blix soon discovered that the university town of Lund held other distractions. To cover necessary expenses they were each given an

A period photograph of Bror's parents and siblings. Bror is sitting on the left in the front row, regarding the photographer with a good deal of suspicion. His oldest brother, Carl, has Bror's twin brother on his lap, and to his right is his mother, Clara, sister Ellen, and father, Frederick. Thyra is in the middle. Marta is standing next to her and Agnes is seated in front of them.

The twins Hans, to the left, and Bror looked very much alike and his father, Frederick, often teased people who wanted to know who was who by saying, "That's Bror [brother] and that's his bror [brother]."

allowance of 100 kronor a month (equivalent today to about $150) to be strictly accounted for. Their accounting of expenditure usually ran thus:

Received	100.00	
To pens, ink, erasers, etc.		1.85
To this and that		98.15
	100.00	100.00

In the beginning they boarded with a family, but they were later allowed the freedom of a small apartment and a limited account with the family grocer. The twins lost no time in charming him into charging their father only for the obviously necessary commodities and hiding details of their more exotic fare, such as champagne, *fois gras,* and candied fruits. Unaware of these machinations, the grocer's assistant billed the baron for everything, including a case of champagne. Their father's only comment was, "Champagne? Why only half bottles?"

At fifteen, Blix and Hans were introduced to Copenhagen's demimonde society in the traditional way: they were each given 100 kronor and the baron's blessing. In those days it was not uncommon for wealthy gentlemen to keep a mistress. When it became necessary to end an affair, the break was usually conducted in the most courteous manner on both sides; the man expressed his undying love but deep regret, and inquired of his mistress as to the terms of a suitable settlement. She would demurely acquiesce and reply, "1,000 kronor and the furniture." It was the standard fee of the day.

Their father's kindness over this introduction to the world of "grown-ups" made the two boys decide to surprise him with an invitation to lunch at one of Copenhagen's better restaurants. To ensure the right venue, they set off ahead of time with their coveted savings to reconnoiter the city. The trip turned into a free-spending affair that soon parted the twins from their wealth. The following day, the impecunious pair wrested with their consciences to devise a way out of this embarrassing predicament, since the lunch could not be cancelled at this stage. With youthful optimism, they decided, "Something will turn up."

Lunch was delightful, and the baron, proud in the company of his two grown sons, thoroughly enjoyed himself. When the time came to settle up, it was all too apparent to the boys that they could not pay the bill. Blix abruptly got

The brothers were taught to use guns at an early age and their meager allowances were stretched by "poaching" rabbits and selling them to local butchers. The picture dates from 1898.

to his feet and left the table. A little later he reappeared, wearing an artful and satisfied smile. The bill was settled and the trio rose to collect coats and hats and to leave. The baron's expensive fur coat was missing. Blix, during his brief absence, had snatched the coat, hurried across the street to a friendly pawnbroker, and secured enough ready cash in the nick of time. Explanations had to be made. Their father laughed at what he took to be a practical joke and went and redeemed his fur coat.

Some years later, the baron was to return to the same restaurant, only to be barred entry. The dining room had been taken over for a private party. On inquiring, he learned that it was for Blix and Hans, to which he said, "Oh, my two sons! In that case, let me in, as I shall end up paying for the whole damn lot!"

The twins' scholastic efforts were no match for their appetite and stamina in pursuit of women, shooting, drinking, and dancing. In those days, an estate always passed on to the eldest son; younger sons were expected to join the cavalry. However, it was essential to have finished school in order to gain entry. This eventually dawned on Hans, who did pass his exams and entered cavalry school.

Like his father, Hans was an outstanding horseman and cut a dashing figure in uniform. He learned to fly and took himself off to race meetings in his own aeroplane. These "manly" attributes endeared him to women, who fell easily under his spell. His lifestyle, well molded during his school days with Blix, did not change. His extravagances were notorious. To this day, the mess bill in his regiment has not been exceeded. Sadly, he crashed his aeroplane in 1917, leaving behind a widow and infant son.*

*Hans's son, inheriting his father's horsemanship, took the Olympic Gold Medal in the three-day event at Helsingfors in 1952.

Nasbyholm, the estate where Bror was born.

Much to his parents' regret, Blix never went into the army. It would hardly have suited him, for although he was a good rider, he was never a great horseman. He would have loathed the tedium of drill and restrictions that were part of the life of an officer. His heart belonged to the country and the sport it offered.

Lacking a student's commitment, Blix struggled through agricultural college at Alnarp and was appointed manager of Stjerneholm, a farm under Nasbyholm. The farm had a good dairy herd, and Blix acquired a sound working knowledge. He was helped by his father, himself a keen stockman, who visited regularly to advise and exchange new ideas.

On one occasion when Blix was out, the maid offered the

baron some coffee. A little later she reappeared, embarrassed. "I'm sorry, sir. I cannot serve you coffee as we've run out of brandy."

Sometimes tiring of these rural pursuits, Blix would hanker after the bacchanalian diversions of former days. These inevitably cost money. Secretly summoning the butcher, he would tell him to choose a cow and fill its empty stall with a pile of straw so that the animal would not be missed. The transaction complete, Blix would take off for Copenhagen.

His father never really got angry with him. It was impossible. Although it has been said that Blix had the morals of a stoat, he was certainly adored by his family and loved by his friends.

Hunting in 1911 with Charlotte (Lotti) Wachtmeister of Trolle-Ljungby. Bror was very much smitten by her and it's not unlikely that his engagement to Tanne was a result of Lotti's hesitation to commit herself.

I think Blix was the only person in the world who truly believed that when he signed a bill it had been paid for.

—KRISTER KUYLENSTIERNA

Two

Tanne and Blix (Denmark/Sweden)

KAREN DINESEN, known to family and friends as Tanne, and the Blixen twins had known each other from childhood. Blix's mother and Tanne's father were cousins. While Tanne was still very young, her father took his life as a result of having contracted syphilis while in America, where he had lived as a young man with the Sioux and Pawnee Indian tribes of Nebraska. He wrote a book about his life with them under the pen name "Boganis," which means hazelnut in Chippewa Indian.

Tanne had been out of the Scandinavian social swing for some years, leading a bohemian life in Copenhagen, Paris, and Rome—studying art and living among poets, intellectuals, and artists. She returned home at the age of twenty-six to find all her women friends married, and her life in the country as daughter of the house restricted and dull.

Around this time, Blix began to find being manager of a small farm frustrating. He had fallen in love with seventeen-year-old Princess Margareta, daughter of Prince Carl and King Gustaf VI's niece, but she had chosen instead to marry

Prince Axel of Denmark. Tanne, too, had been turned down by Blix's twin brother, Hans.

At this point their mutual uncle, Mogens Frijs, was in Sweden on a visit from Kenya, where he had land at Naivasha. His enthusiasm for the country sparked in them an idea to escape the confines of their present lives.

For Blix, Africa spelled adventure. Frijs had stressed that Kenya was the place in which a young man could make his mark, and possibly his fortune too. Men with capital were being encouraged to settle and invest in its future. Blix lacked the capital. Perhaps it was at this moment that Tanne made a suggestion. If they were to marry, her family could provide the necessary money.

For Tanne's romantic nature, Africa aroused an intense curiosity, and the idea of becoming a Baroness appealed to her very strongly. It would imply an immediate status, an acknowledged proof that she was part of that charmed inner circle of carefree, secure nobility. It would bring immediate recognition of her place in the hierarchy. She would be financially secure through her own family, but money alone was not enough. She would marry Blix. It was as if she had composed a perfectly balanced design. The pieces fitted so easily: marriage, title, and a new and exciting future.

Although it was one of convenience, their marriage was built on friendship and affection. For the present, they set aside the reality of their fundamentally opposite temperaments. Tanne neither shared his wild drinking sprees nor approved of his open womanizing, while Blix had no desire to understand Tanne's more artistic and intellectual bent. She was of a contrary nature, usually opting for the way least expected of her. Blix predictably took the way that offered least resistance.

Both families were dismayed, Tanne's in particular, by the announcement of their intentions. From her sojourn at art schools, Tanne had picked up such modern habits as smoking

Blix and Tanne

and wearing makeup, and her mother had hoped she would settle down nearer to home with a steady and hard-working landowner. Blix's family, on the other hand, was disappointed he had not chosen someone from his own background, and they found Tanne rather aloof. However, Blix's nieces and nephews looked forward to her visits to Nasbyholm, anticipating the imaginative fairy tales and stories she entertained them with.

This imaginative trait was the one thread Blix and Tanne shared in common. Between them they conjured up a dream. Their dream, however, was founded on the beneficence of

Tanne's uncle, her mother's brother, Aage Westenholz. Since her father's death, Westenholz had become the family advisor and trustee. He agreed to advance the money for the land purchase in Kenya.

A bond of dependence grew between Blix and Tanne. In this new venture they became accomplices, throwing in their lot with the unknown.

Myself, I feel like a lark high in the sky enjoying all the splendours of Africa.

—Bror Blixen

Three

Kenya and Lord Delamere

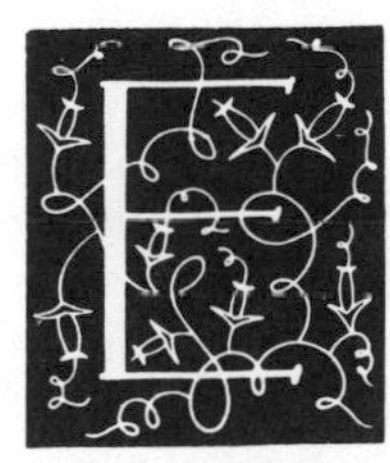

UROPEAN SETTLEMENT in Kenya had first been made possible by the vision of Hugh Cholmondeley, third Baron Delamere.

At the age of twenty-seven, Delamere came to East Africa from the north. Guided by rudimentary sketch maps drawn by the only two explorers to have returned from that vast semidesert waste south of Somaliland, he crossed over one thousand miles, with a handful of Somali guides and his young English friend, Dr. A. E. Atkinson. In 1896 his caravan of two hundred camels, laden with rifles, ammunition, instruments, tents, bales of calico cloth, and colored beads, traveled south from Berbera into Abyssinia, as far as Lugh. From there he turned west roughly along the Kenya-Ethiopian border, hooking south on a direct line to Marsabit, east of Lake Rudolf, skirting its southern shore down the Turkwell River to Lake Baringo, and reaching the Laikipia plateau in August 1897.

To men accustomed to a year's wandering beneath rainless skies, over stony deserts and dry water courses, Laikipia's cool heights and rolling plains, contrasting with the forested slopes of snow-capped Mount Kenya and the Aberdares, must have been intoxicating. Stranger still—unlike the thorn and scrub deserts where he had encountered Somali, Gall, Boran, Rendille, Turkana, and Samburu tribes—here Delamere encountered no one. The land was unoccupied. (In 1891 the Laikipia clan of the Maasai tribe had been annihilated by the Purko clan, and their cattle had been wiped out by Rinderpest plague the previous year.) With his previous experience in Australia and New Zealand, this first sight of fertile land, unused potential, sowed the seeds for the idea of its future settlement and development by people of his own race.

In 1899, a year after his arrival home, he married Lady Florence Cole, daughter of the Earl of Enniskillen, and returned with his wife to Kenya that same year from a bird-collecting trip for the British Museum. This time he traveled up country from Mombasa to Nairobi on the bi-weekly Imperial Railway, which had got as far as the Kikuyu Escarpment. It was during this trip that the idea of white settlement was first discussed in earnest. Sir Charles Eliot, a scholar and linguist, and the British Commissioner realized, like Delamere, that not only was the soil suitable, the climate healthy, and the land unoccupied but there was the question of an expensive railway to be serviced and utilized. Settlement was an economic necessity, and Eliot accordingly persuaded the Foreign Office, which had been reluctant to deal with the land question, to complete the railway.

The first inducements to attract settlers were inadequate, restricted by muddled bureaucratic rules and regulations. During the couple's second trip (his third), on a visit to the commissioner's office Delamere learned of the negligible success Eliot's efforts had so far engendered. It was then proposed that Delamere himself promote and encourage settlement on the government's behalf.

At that period, there were less than a dozen settlers; this increased to one hundred by mid-1903. Their attempts to grow fruit and vegetables in and around the railhead at Nairobi appeared at first successful, but in time these suffered bug and fly infestations. Livestock fared no better. From these small experiments, Delamere realized that future settlers must be men of capital, able to sustain experimentation on a large scale. To prove to the world that Kenya could take its place among other thriving colonies, Delamere set himself up as the first capitalist-adventurer, often borrowing heavily on his English estates to achieve his end.

This determination to create an English extension was further accelerated as a result of the British government's hasty attempts to fill the gap. It arbitrarily invited first a Finnish settlement, rejected by the Finns in 1902, then an Indian settlement, and finally one by Russian and Polish Jews, victims of persecution.

This last idea had first come to Joseph Chamberlain, a Zionist sympathizer, on a visit in 1902. Similarly struck by the country's fertile emptiness, he advocated a Jewish Settlement Scheme, and a definite offer of five thousand square miles for a Jewish self-governed settlement under British protection was made to the Zionist leader, Dr. Theodor Herzl, in Basle. However, the Russian and Polish Jews were themselves totally opposed to the idea of a halfway house to the "promised land." It had to be Palestine or nothing.

Early settlers, restricted to survey and rent payments and bogged down by bureaucratic delays to land entitlement, were equally incensed, finding it incomprehensible that their own government should rob them of future promise and hand part of their country over to foreigners. An angry mob convened in Nairobi and formed a committee, of which Delamere was chairman, to squash the proposal. With a steady stream of new arrivals, Eliot, who had been previously open-minded on settlement, now felt the settlers had a point and informed the Foreign Office accordingly.

However, the final analysis was concluded on a visit to the area by a Zionist commission, who set off by train to Londiani with a couple of settlers to pave the way. They arrived at the top of the Uasin Gishu plateau with blistered feet and aching backs, to camp at the edge of the forest. Here they were welcomed by a band of Maasai warriors in warlike mood and attire who left only after some deft persuasion. At night their peace was disturbed by crashing elephants and rhinoceros and sniffing and prowling lions—after the delegation had been entertained by campfire stories of the Maneaters of Tsavo. The commission stayed only three days, then returned to London to report that the district was most unsuited to Russian and Polish refugees. The Zionist Congress formally rejected the offer in 1905.

Delamere's first application for land at Laikipia was turned down because it was too far from the railway and administration centers. His second choice, a concession of one hundred thousand acres running from the Aberdares to Naivasha, was similarly refused, on the grounds that it would interfere with the Maasai. He then asked for a block in the Rift Valley between Njoro and the Molo River, well west of the Maasai, who actually shunned the area because their cattle could not survive there. (The reason—lack of essential minerals—did not become apparent until the 1920s.) He made this his first home in Africa, which he called Equator Ranch.

Over the next few years, he would experiment with sheep, cattle, wheat, maize, ostrich, citrus, and wattle bark by importing pedigree stock, machinery, fencing, and implements from England, Australia, and New Zealand. He experienced setback after setback. Livestock was decimated by tick, worm, and fly-borne disease as well as thefts and marauding lions. Wheat and maize broke down to rust, aphids, and, later, swarms of locust capable of devouring an entire crop within seconds. Undeterred, he created a plant-breeding station, crossed imported cattle and sheep with native Boran and Maasai stock, and formed companies to market and process agricultural products.

Delamere was known for his short temper. He had no time for shirkers, but he was immensely generous to those who

A street scene from Nairobi celebrating the end of World War I. The banners fly along the main street lined with people anticipating the victory parade.

worked loyally for him. A great admirer of the Maasai, he learned to speak their language fluently and indulged their cattle-thieving pastimes, which he felt resulted naturally from a firm belief that they were the appointed keepers of God's cattle.

When the policy restricting Maasai movements came into question, and over which Eliot resigned, Delamere came up with the idea of combining a Maasai reserve with a game reserve—the Maasai did not eat game—thus protecting the game without tying up additional land otherwise suitable for development. In 1904, two separate reserves came into being: the Laikipia plateau, and the Maasai Mara, lying south of the railway as far as the German border of Tanganyika. The Maasai later chose to reunite with the southern clan, and Laikipia was once more open to settlement.

Delamere took up the settlers' cause with tireless energy and became their natural leader. As a member of the Legislative Council, formed in 1907, he fought for their rights on land entitlement, railway taxes, labor, and Indian questions. This necessitated frequent trips to Nairobi, during which he left the running of the farm to his wife. On one occasion, he flagged down the train and boarded with a bull terrier and her litter, which prompted the station master to telegraph his superior: "The lord is on the train with one bitch and four sons of bitches. No ticket. Please collect." In those days, tickets were rarely bought in advance. The train stopped for anyone who waved vigorously enough, and the driver and engineer might themselves stop the train for a day's shooting. Traveling up from Mombasa, Delamere, who was furious by the delay of having to wait for the shooting party to return, simply engaged the services of the African assistant, who had never driven a train before, and left the amazed engineer and driver to find their own way back.

Delamere never did anything by half measure. He partied as vigorously as he debated, sometimes to the detriment of his own property. Wild rickshaw races, with participants toting guns and popping streetlights, were often led by Delamere, hunched over the reins, shoulder-length hair flying out from under his wide slouch hat.

Close on Delamere's heels came his wife's brothers, Galbraith and Berkeley Cole. Galbraith first settled on a grant of fifty thousand acres at Laikipia in 1903, carrying his dismantled wagons over the escarpment. As a result of the Maasai Reserve treaty, he was moved off. He then acquired thirty thousand acres at Gilgil, called Kekopey, which neighbored on Delamere's second land holding, Soysambu Ranch, to which Delamere ultimately moved to live in 1910, following stock failures at Njoro. Galbraith and Delamere built up the first stock of wool sheep, importing New Zealand Merino rams, which they crossed with native Maasai sheep. Although in two decades Galbraith had established a herd of thirty thousand Merino crosses, 90 percent of the lambs were lost in that first year. Stock theft was a major hazard. Galbraith owed a spell of deportation in 1911 to having taken the law, which was unforthcoming, into his own hands and fatally wounding a Kikuyu rustler he had surprised skinning a precious Merino import. Returning briefly, disguised as a Somali, Galbraith was quickly smuggled out by Berkeley, with the help of friends in the government capable of unorthodox administration. War intervened, and he returned in 1914.

In 1917, Galbraith married Eleanor Balfour in London. He had met her on a rare visit to Nairobi the previous year. She was the daughter of the second Earl of Balfour and niece of former Prime Minister Arthur Balfour. She shared with Galbraith the years of struggle wrought by renewed attacks of stock disease, drought, locusts, and finally the increasingly acute pain of rheumatoid arthritis, with which her husband had been plagued from an early age. They returned to England in 1927 for treatment. Confined to a wheelchair, he could only dream of returning to Kekopey to look out once again on its familiar plains and lake; to see Jama Farah, his Somali servant who had cared for him for so long; "to die where I can hear the zebra barking." His wish was ironically fulfilled two years later. Nell, as his wife was known, loaded the revolver and walked out with the dogs. Jama Farah supported his withered arm and witnessed Galbraith's final brave gesture. Nell was left to run the two farms.

His brother, Berkeley Cole, took up land at Naro Moru on the slopes of Mount Kenya. Good-looking and blessed with a quick Irish wit and charm, he never married, preferring the free-spirited and unfettered company of a Somali mistress. He was a good friend of another bachelor and fellow Etonian, Denys Finch-Hatton, who subsequently became Tanne Blixen's lover.

I only respect one God and two mortals: Allah and the Baron and Baroness Blixen.

—Farah Aden

Four

Tanne: 1913–1922

T THE BEGINNING OF 1913, Blix left Europe, ahead of Tanne, to take possession of the land they had bought, unseen, through a land agent. The idea was to start a dairy herd. He stayed at the Norfolk Hotel in Nairobi, the pivotal point of contact for any new settler, hunter, adventurer, or government official. Blix was soon persuaded to experiment with coffee rather than cattle. Coffee had been successfully established north of Nairobi at Thika and at St. Austins (now part of Nairobi's western suburb), where it was grown by White Fathers, missionaries, who had introduced it in 1896. A fellow Swede, Ake Sjogren further persuaded him to offload his semideveloped concern of 750 acres in exchange for 4,500 acres of undeveloped land south of Nairobi at the foot of the Ngong Hills. Not surprisingly, Tanne's and Blix's families became alarmed at this sudden change of plans. Skillfully using the same arguments others had used on him, Blix won them over to the idea that coffee, rather than cattle, was the future.

The Europeans who came to settle after the first decade of

the century were from landed stock, for the most part gentlemen and aristocrats. They were financially independent. Many had strong reasons to leave their comfortable lives in Europe, desirous either of being free of civilization's restrictive codes or of avoiding or escaping scandal. The country attracted sportsmen, entrepreneurs, adventurers, a few devoted naturalists, and those who merely believed the grass to be greener. Of course not all those who came before World War I were aristocrats or nurtured on the playing fields of Eton, but these people did set the tone. They played hard and worked hard, never excusing or regretting. They made a life, if not a living, and lived that life to the fullest. They all possessed a common bond: independence, tenacity, ambition, and fearlessness. Blix was one of them.

By the time Blix arrived, a modicum of order had been created out of a primitive and bare beginning. The country was slowly making headway. However, each new block of land that was taken up had to be broken and tamed despite the same pitfalls that befell earlier settlers, like Delamere ten years before.

The farm Blix bought lay about twelve miles outside Nairobi and was at over 6,000 feet elevation. Blix moved into the manager's house, a stone house surrounded by a deep wooden veranda on the banks of the Mbagathi River—"stream" would be more apt, for in times of drought it barely ran at all. The house was surrounded by an indigenous forest of Croton, wild fig (Mgumu), and the lilac-flowering Cape Chestnut. Its inhabitants were the Sykes and Colobus monkey, buffalo, bushbuck, and leopard. The plains to the east abounded with lion, zebra, wildebeest, rhinoceros, and gazelle. The house looked south to the Ngong Hills, crowned by four distinct rounded peaks, broken by forested valleys running down to meet rolling hills and more wooded valleys.

Blix's first task was to find enough laborers to clear the land. These were not easily available, for although his Maasai neighbors south of the river were closer at hand, they were not inclined to work the land, preferring to take on the more traditional role of cattle herders. This meant Blix had to travel long distances and spend days negotiating with tribal chiefs and administrative heads. In time, he did recruit enough men to start. The recruits were mainly of the Kikuyu tribe. They arrived with their families to settle on a few acres of land in return for the services, and they were known as "squatters." They built the traditional mud and daub, thatched rondavels, whose roofs steamed with the all-pervasive smell of wood smoke in the early morning chill.

Clearing trees and bush was a laborious and drawn-out affair; it entailed not only cutting down the trees, but removing each deeply rooted stump by hand. Once the land was cleared, it had to be plowed. This was done by teams of six or eight oxen, which had been broken and trained by Dutch South Africans, with the experience of generations of Voortrekkers. Deep holes were then dug at staked intervals and the coffee seedlings inserted vertically, taking care to avoid bending the crucial tap root. Planting was done in the rains; the black, clay soil clogged the cart wheels and oozed between fingers and toes as each seedling was prodded and stamped into the ground. The work was supervised by Blix and six European managers, among whom were the Swedes Ake Bursell, Emil Holmberg, and Ture Rundgren.

In the meantime, Tanne was planning her departure from Denmark. Her preparations included steamer trunks filled with silver, crystal, china, furniture, linen, paintings, jewelry, carpets, grandfather clocks, bound books, and a wardrobe of the very latest in fashionable dress. She would arrive with all the outward signs of her exalted position.

Just before Tanne's arrival, Blix wrote to his sister Ellen:

> Tomorrow Tanne will be arriving with Prince Wilhelm and Lewenhaupt and it is of course an important day in one's life. I can think of no better place to receive one's fiancée. I am

> planning to take her up to Naivasha to Uncle Mogen's place where I have arranged a lion gallop using Paul Rainey's dogs.* I cannot think of a better introduction to the Wild!

On January 13, 1914, Tanne arrived at Mombasa with Prince Wilhelm, brother of Sweden's future King Gustaf VI, and his companion Count Lewenhaupt. She was met by Blix and the Swedish consul, who was to convey the Prince and Lewenhaupt to Nairobi, where they were the guests of the American millionaire Northrup McMillan, on whose ranch they would be hunting. Prince Wilhelm later bought land at Rosslyn, which is today a suburb west of Nairobi. Another fellow passenger, whose name was to become famous a few months hence, was Lieutenant Colonel Paul von Lettow-Vorbeck. He was to command the German East African forces at the outbreak of the war. Tanne and he had become very close during the boat's passage out, and it has been hinted they were lovers.

The following day, the fourteenth, Blix and Tanne were married quietly in Mombasa. Prince Wilhelm and Count Lewenhaupt were in attendance. The wedding party then boarded the special Nairobi-bound train arranged for the royal visitors by the governor, Sir Henry Belfield.

At Nairobi they were met by the farm manager. What excitement! They would soon be on their way to the new farm. The buggy, drawn by six mules, jogged out of the station forecourt, leaving behind Nairobi's crowded and colorful bazaars for the clear, bright morning's sunshine.

As they went along, Blix pointed out game, recounted adventures on previous journeys—here an axle had broken and he had to chase the wheel for miles down the hill; there, at a river crossing, he had come across a lion. His face was

*Paul Rainey, an American, brought the first pack of lion dogs out. He was to have sent a guide to show them the way, but the guide never appeared. It was probably just as well, for Blix's Austrian friend, Fritz Schindelar, was pulled from his horse that day and badly mauled by lion. He died a week later.

Blix taught Tanne to handle guns and she developed into an excellent shot. Like most newcomers she was eager to fell as many big game animals as possible. This fervor subsequently cooled and later on she hunted only in order to feed her many employees.

alight with the joy of sharing with Tanne the life he had come to love. Her excitement deepened as they neared the hills beyond, a deep purple ridge hung with fluffy white clouds. Blix wondered how Tanne would settle into this new life, to its people; all was so different from the tidy and ordered existence she had left behind. He hoped she would be as enthusiastic and optimistic about their future as he, and that the progress he had made would please her.

He need not have worried. She took to the country and immediately developed a close rapport with its people. Coming to a land of stark contrast, as from day to night, she felt reborn.

That spring of 1914, they had good rains and planted a substantial amount of coffee. Things had not gone so well at the beginning of the year. Blix, writing again to his sister, recounted some of the problems they had to face:

> All the africans have smallpox. Holmberg is suffering from sunstroke, Rundgren from smallpox, and Mr. Grieve accidentally shot himself in the face a couple of days ago which has not improved his already untidy appearance. Two cows and two oxen died last night of East Coast Fever. But I feel as a lark, high in the sky. I am really enjoying all the splendour of Africa. I am not sure what it is. I suppose just being away from gossip and nagging. To set foot on land never ploughed before, to walk in forests that have known neither axe nor saw. A country in its cradle, with an ideal climate and tremendous potential.

Blix already had the taste for big-game hunting and was eager to introduce Tanne to safari life. The coffee would take five years to mature. There was time to visit new friends and experience new country.

Time, however, was not on their side. War broke out during August of that year. At that stage, no one in Kenya knew what it would mean for them. It all seemed so far away, and it was hoped that Germany and England would battle on their own shores. An untimely bombardment of German ships in Dar-es-Salaam Harbor in Tanganyika precipitated the issue. German nationals were immediately interned. Men of all nationalities and description converged on Nairobi, eager to join up, but there were no units to join. A group of Boer farmers from the Uasin Gishu plateau formed themselves into a regiment called the Plateau South Africans, a generous gesture considering the Boer War was not long behind them. Other regiments materialized, to finally be merged into the East African Mounted Rifles. Each man arrived equipped with whatever he could lay his hands on: rifles ranging from double-barrel elephant guns to shotguns, assorted ammunition, water-bottles and hip flasks, skinning and kitchen knives. There were no uniforms. Each man pleased himself in bush khaki shorts or britches, tennis shoes or riding boots. Eight hundred Somalis offered their services and were organized into a mounted unit under Berkeley Cole.

The untenable German-Tanganyika border ran undefended for two hundred miles, mostly through Maasai Reserve country. All the administrative posts followed the railway line further north. It was decided to form an intelligence department, headed by the chief game warden, a Captain Woosnam, whose section already had a network of informers to enforce game laws. Delamere, with his invaluable knowledge of the Maasai, was appointed commanding officer on the Maasai border. In conjunction with Delamere, there were, among others, Bill Judd, a professional hunter; a Boer by the name of Postma; and the Swedes, Ture Rundgren, Nils Fjastad, and Blix. They each took up position at hastily assembled points or one-man trading centers along the line.

Woosnam told Blix to organize everything himself, requisitioning any equipment he might need. A haphazard line of communication evolved, using motorcycles, bicycles, and a string of native runners. Others used carrier pigeons, with mixed results, since many pigeons were caught by birds of

Blix and Bursell joined Lord Delamere's search patrols. At their disposal they had a vehicle that soon proved unfit for the terrain in which they were forced to operate.

prey. On one occasion, two pigeons homed in totally devoid of plumage. One way or another, all the pigeons were eventually killed, lost in action presumably, without even the honor of being decorated posthumously. Blix's assortment of carriers fared somewhat better, relaying intelligence to the end station at Kijabe.

A member of the South African cavalry platoon, on loan to

guard Delamere's base camp, galloped into Blix's camp one day in a great state of excitement, announcing that Delamere's fly-camp was under attack by German artillery. (A fly-camp was a more temporary facility than a fully stocked base camp.) Blix relayed the report to his commanding officer and offered his services. He did, however, mention that Delamere's camp, which he had visited the previous evening, was manned only by a handful of Maasai morans (young warriors); it was highly improbable that the Germans would waste their fire on such a small and unimportant enclave. Blix also diplomatically pointed out that the noise of artillery could have been confused with that of a freak thunderstorm, which was often experienced in the area around that time of year. "Look, man! I fought in the Boer War and bloody well know the difference between artillery and thunder!" barked the CO.

In preparation for the counterattack, Blix passed around his hip flask, and the South Africans produced their Bibles for a silent prayer. They set off armed to the teeth in anticipation of the enemy. Halfway there, Blix intercepted a couple of dispatch runners who told him they had left Delamere's camp that morning in a heavy thunderstorm! The South Africans refused to believe these "kaffir" lies and set off to complete their mission. Blix left them to it and went home.

Even Tanne had been enlisted into Blix's contingent. She was put in charge of supplies at the Kijabe link station. From there she organized the transport of supplies to the line of communication. On her first run she had engaged the services of a young South African, Klapprot, to oversee the ox wagons. The poor man was taken for a German by the now-hysterical authorities and arrested. Tanne was left to take charge herself. It was a wonder that she was not arrested herself, for her friendship with the dreaded von Lettow was well known.

During this first run, Tanne showed immense fortitude and proved herself to be a brave woman. On foot, with forty oxen, she covered the eighty miles between Kijabe and Narok in four days.

On the third evening, as they were outspanning, two of the oxen were attacked by lion. The frightened teamsters disappeared. Tanne, unarmed, was left to face the marauders alone. Brandishing a heavy stock whip, she lashed out at the lion. He turned tail and ran.

On another run, Blix suddenly appeared in camp. He had come down with bad dysentery and taken a few days' leave. He had followed Tanne's tracks for two days. She relates in one of her letters, "He was so stiff we had to fold him together. He had slept in a Maasai Manyatta and gone without food."

The whole contingent was finally withdrawn when Delamere became ill and left for England. Blix returned to Nairobi at the end of the year to find that Woosnam had been transferred. Blix was left to pay for the past year's efforts out of his own pocket, as well the expenses of Tanne's supply runs. The authorities had become more reluctant to engage non-soldiers, and most of the settler forces were disbanded. When he returned to the farm, Blix discovered that all his oxen and wagons had been commandeered by the government. It was also evident they no longer needed him. In some quarters there was a growing antipathy toward foreigners. "Foreigner" implied anyone who was not English.

One evening Blix was sitting on the veranda of the Norfolk Hotel having a drink with Walter Shapley, a prominent lawyer with a marked Teutonic appearance, and Arnold Meyer, editor of the *East African Standard* newspaper, born a

Tanne aided Blix on several occasions by bringing supplies, by ox-drawn wagons, to the patrols under his command.

At the outset of their residence in Kenya, Tanne and Blix seemed to enjoy getting dressed up rather than merely getting dressed. Bursell is in the middle.

German Jew and now a naturalized British subject. Dark, hostile looks in their direction caused Shapley, a man of humor, to react in his unmistakable, booming voice: "We seem to be the three most suspicious characters here this evening. You, Meyer, are German. I look like one, and Blix here, God knows what he is!"

At the beginning of 1915, the outlook for the farm was bleak. The short rains had failed, resulting in severe drought. The labor force had been drastically reduced, but there was little Blix and Tanne could do about it. Their Maasai neighbors, too, were badly hit, with cattle dying in thousands from lack of water and good grazing. Tanne became unwell. Blix was concerned, writing at length to her mother. He eventually persuaded her to go with their mutual friend, Helge Fagerskiold, on a safari to the Aberdares and Mount Kenya, where he hoped the change of air would cure her. She got no better, and was advised by a doctor in Nairobi to travel home to Denmark.

It was during this period in their lives that it has been said Tanne contracted syphilis. All the doctors I have consulted emerge with different theories about it. No one can speak with real authority.

Tanne's father is supposed to have discovered syphilis in himself after living in America among the Indians of Nebraska. It was then thought that syphilis was incurable, with insanity the outcome. Was his suicide the despairing gesture of a man without hope?

Perhaps later, the young girl who unearthed the secret of her father's death could have become obsessed with the thought that she carried the disease in her genes. When she got malaria for the first time, and delirium raged in the high temperatures of her fever, did she think she was actually going insane like her father? Did she indeed imagine that she too had syphilis?

In those days, sexual promiscuity was never to be associated with women of good family, so inevitably it was assumed that Blix was responsible for infecting her. But in her Bohemian days in Paris and Rome, Tanne had had passionate friendships with fellow students. Tanne was not a virgin when she married.

On May 15, 1915, Tanne wrote to her mother to say she was on her way to London to see a specialist in tropical diseases. She stressed the fact that her illness must have been due to frequent malarial attacks and subsequent heavy doses of quinine. In the same letter she wrote: "Believe me, I am so upset to leave Bror. . . !" If, as biographers have sought to prove, a doctor did diagnose syphilis, I believe she would not have made so spontaneous a declaration of what sadness their

It was necessary to supply the large work force on the farm with meat, and the ample supply of antelopes and gazelles made the job easier for Blix and Bursell.

separation caused. And as one contemporary doctor observed, "Why did not any of all the other women Blix fooled around with contract it?"

Tanne spent over a year in Denmark with her family. Blix was unable to join her until the middle of 1916.

Nineteen fifteen, the year of her absence, was known as "the Black Year" in Kenya. The British had suffered a series of humiliating defeats, the drought had been devastating, and morale was low. Blix managed to continue to run the farm, although many of his men had been drafted into the Carrier Corps and coffee was not considered a wartime priority.

In November 1916, Blix and Tanne returned to Kenya, via London, sailing on the *Balmoral Castle* around the Cape. They stopped over in South Africa for two weeks to look at farms. There they stayed with the Honorable Joseph Baynes, a great character, who was much taken with Blix's new two-seater car. Blix was impressed by all he saw and began to make plans to expand and diversify their own farm. He hoped to breed pigs and cattle, grow flowers, and, at the coast, sugarcane and coconut palms. Blix's brother-in-law, Gustaf Hamilton, who was to be involved in the sugarcane project, traveled out with them. Blix threw himself wholeheartedly into getting these projects started. Tanne, too, was enthusiastic and encouraged him with the cattle.

Soon after their return, they lost their best manager, Ake Bursell. He had bought land of his own at Ruiru. Bursell certainly had more practical experience than Blix, and he would have been a real asset to them in getting the new venture moving. He also had a more down-to-earth sense of economics than the Blixens, neither of whom had been brought up to handle money. Advisors and trustees had always taken care of the family finances.

The following year, 1917, the main farm house, a two-story building in stone, became vacant. Blix and Tanne moved in. Sjogren had left his library of Swedish books, for which Tanne was greatly indebted. For the moment, busy putting the new house in order with the help of seven Somali servants under the supervision of Farah Aden,* Tanne felt content. But one can sense from their correspondence, over this period, an underlying feeling of unease. It was as if they did not yet feel settled. Blix nursed the hope of making enough money to return to Denmark to buy back Dallund, the original Blixen estate, where his mother still lived on a much reduced scale and acreage.

The war trailed on with little sign of success. The British failed to rout von Lettow, who had become a living legend, both feared and admired. In a renewed effort to improve supply lines, which had grown weaker in the drawn-out pursuit

*Farah, Tanne's personal servant, had been sent to meet her on her initial voyage to Mombasa, at Aden; hence the name Farah Aden. When Tanne left the country for good, Farah stayed on with Blix.

Farah Aden, Tanne's personal servant, had been sent to meet her when she returned from her first trip to Mombasa by Aden; thus the name Farah Aden. When Tanne left the country for good, Farah stayed behind with Blix.

of the German commander, the British increased the Carrier Corps by well over 15,000 African men. These were borrowed mainly from the farms, which, still in their infancy, were thus left short-handed and were brought virtually to a standstill.

Perhaps frustrated by an elusive quarry, by the prolonged rains, and by a general feeling of despair, the community looked for an enemy closer at hand. The small Swedish community became their imagined foe, due mainly to the slanderous pen of a certain W. S. Bromhead, who wrote damning articles in *The Leader*. Among other things, he accused the Blixens of having "tainted" money and German associates; Tanne's shipboard romance had even been talked about. This affected Tanne badly, especially since her brother, Thomas, had joined the Black Watch Regiment of Canada and was fighting in France; in 1918 he received both the British Victoria Cross and the French Croix de Guerre. Blix as usual took it all light-heartedly, but he went to see Bromhead, who at once published a retraction.

The elevation and rarified air of the Kenya Highlands have been said to produce a certain euphoria in its European inhabitants. Blix was no exception to the charms of this charged atmosphere. His gregarious and fun-loving nature propelled him into Nairobi's social swing. If an *affaire* chanced his way, who knows whether Tanne minded? When they married, it had been understood that the marriage would be a working partnership built on friendship and affection. Faithfulness was, after all, a middle-class expectation.

But the farm's isolation weighed heavily on Tanne, especially with Blix away so much. Although she read and painted, she lacked the mental stimulus of kindred souls around her and found herself more dependent on Blix than she had ever thought possible. She had no real friends, and she had little in common with the wives of their farm managers, with the exception of Olga Holmberg. In fact, she had little time for most women, preferring on the whole the company of men.

She was not always left on the farm. Blix and she frequently traveled together up-country to visit and stay with other landowners. Travel then was a laborious affair, with long distances to cover over dusty roads and tracks. Hospitality was commensurate with the effort, and people stayed over for days, sometimes weeks at a time.

Muthaiga Club

One favorite host was Northrup McMillan, whose generous hospitality was as vast as his 350-pound frame. McMillan, a southerner from St. Louis, had arrived in Kenya in 1904, having led an expedition through Abyssinia, partly by Nile steamer, with his friend Major Charles Bulpett, known fondly as "Uncle." Bulpett claimed, without regret, that he had been ruined by the famous courtesan La Belle Otero, who had helped him spend to the tune of £100,000 in six months. He stayed with McMillan and his wife, Lucie, at Juja Ranch for the rest of his life. McMillan was later knighted for his wartime services to Britain.

Reversing the role, the Blixens entertained the Swedish Baron Erik von Otter on the farm at Ngong. In spite of his "foreignness," von Otter was still attached to the King's African Rifles. Tall and good-looking, he had gained a remarkable reputation in the army, especially among his African *askaris* (soldiers), whose company he preferred. He was an excellent shot and had acquired the name "risasi moja" (one shot). He and Tanne became close friends through their common interest in the Koran and Islamic culture. Unlike Chris-

tians, Muslims have no concept of sin; Tanne felt this was altogether a more pragmatic and realistic view. With this concept in mind, she and von Otter went on safari together.

On her return she writes at length to her mother of von Otter's charms, adding in the letter:

> I want you all that believe in Bror, not to judge him as you would others. He must have his liberty and be what he is in order to achieve what he is most capable of. It is my utmost wish that you blind yourselves to Bror for another two or three years so that even if 'he steals twopence from a blind beggar with which to buy poison for his mother', you will say, 'It was only his high spirits.'

Later that year, while Blix was visiting their Uasin Gishu farm, Tanne met Denys Finch-Hatton for the first time, at Muthaiga Club.

Muthaiga Club existed as the town seat of the up-country settler, a civilized extension to his own home. With the growing antipathy between settler and administration, the need arose for a separate club. Built from large blocks of stone, covered with roseate pebbledash, it was run along the lines of a smart London club. It was, however, unique, unlike any other club anywhere in the world. It combined certain standards of good breeding with the freedom of behavior that prevails when people know themselves to be securely marked by birth and status. In the most cosmopolitan fashion, its doors were open to all Europeans with the same outlook, and urbanity, wit, and charm. Its doric columns added a certain glitter to the parade of contrasts. Beautiful, adventurous young women mixed with older and wiser hands. Pale-faced new arrivals and hunting guests stood out against hunters and farmers, who were characterized by sunbaked skins as tough as their well-worn saddle bags and crumpled khaki bush jackets jingling with ammunition. Newcomers were quick to learn that good form required them to dress down by day. By night, the same actors reappeared transformed in glittering evening wear and jewels.

Secluded bush and farm life caused people to break out when they could. Parties were rowdy affairs. The club had a rule, still in force today, that a member is entitled to damage any loose property as long as he pays double its value. Members were admonished not for having ended the evening wrapped around a chandelier but for being in arrears with their bills. Payments were transacted on colored chits; cash never passed hands. Blix's name came up once before the committee in this connection, but a debate on whether to import Spanish as well as French olives totally eclipsed his probable reprimand.

When Tanne met Finch-Hatton, she was enchanted. Writing again to her mother, she explains that he, like the Cole brothers and Delamere, was one of the early settlers. "They are so much better sort than the later ones." However, Finch-Hatton not only appealed to Tanne's snobbish side. He was good-looking, charming, intelligent, and cultivated. In recent years, the notion that they were lovers has captivated

It must have been confusing to the local population to be forced to participate in the war between Germans and Englishmen. Von Lettow-Vorbeck nevertheless succeeded in gathering a loyal force of local soldiers within a short time and training them to become excellent soldiers who were regarded with both respect and fear by their opponents. Here Finch-Hatton interrogates a soldier who is suspected of giving valuable information to the German forces.

writers of romance. People who knew him remember him as a man who appealed to men and women alike. He was loved by everyone. Essentially, they shared a deep love of Africa, books, and music. She had at last found a kindred spirit. Blix was delighted, even flattered that she should be attracted to a man he both liked and admired. Blix was never a jealous man.

The year 1918 was financially disastrous. The long rains failed. Waterholes dried up. Famine was followed by plague, and people died by the thousands. The drought did not spare the Blixens' coffee. Blaming the losses on Blix's mismanagement, Aage Westenholz, still controlling the money, turned the farm into a company, with himself as chairman and the shares going to Tanne's family members. It was a rather harsh decision, considering that Blix's family had invested a considerable amount of money in the farm as well.

Although both Tanne and Blix were extravagant in the extreme, Blix worked hard to make money. With nothing coming off their own farm, they moved to Naivasha to plow 2,000 acres for Delamere. During their stay, Tanne had a bad fall riding and developed an infection. It was treated by the unconventional Dr. Roland W. Burkitt, whose method of reducing Tanne's temperature involved wrapping her in a wet blanket and driving her at full speed through the cold night air.

Then, at last, the war was over. The country's social life gathered momentum, and the Blixens' "German ties" were soon forgotten. They found themselves invited out and entertained once again. To Tanne's delight, Finch-Hatton returned from Egypt, where he had been learning to fly. The first rains fell, and life was born anew.

In January 1919, Denys Finch-Hatton took Tanne alone on safari with him to Mount Kenya. It is curious that at this stage Blix and Tanne continued to discuss their future in Kenya. Their social positions had changed radically since the armistice. In spite of the antipathy shown them during the war, they now felt accepted and very much a part of the country. Blix told Tanne that even if he made no money out of the venture, he would be satisfied to have participated in molding the future of Kenya.

Finch-Hatton and Berkeley Cole were frequent visitors, enjoying a comfortable and beautifully appointed house, a contrast to their rough bachelor quarters. Berkeley would arrive loaded down with turkeys' eggs and oranges from his farm, cases of vintage wine and champagne, and books and records from Europe. What seemed to be the mid-morning crack of rifle fire often turned out to be Berkeley popping champagne corks in the forest.

The love of such an idyllic existence was not shared by Tanne's family, now despairing of the losses in which the African adventure was involving them. The family continued to pour in money, at the irreparable cost of selling off parcels of Dinesen Danish sea-front property. In August 1919, the Blixens set sail for Europe to confront and report to the Danish shareholders. This did not prevent them from spending much time and money on the way.

Traveling in style, Tanne brought with her a young Somali servant. Heads turned to watch as she walked proud and erect ahead of him. In London, they stayed at the Carlton, where Geoffrey Buxton, a friend from Kenya, organized a small dinner party. Blix went alone. Among the guests were Buxton's cousin, Ben Birkbeck, and his wife Cockie. Cockie loved parties and was without a doubt a lively member of any gathering. She had an arch sense of humor and a predilection for off-color music hall songs. She later became Blix's second wife.

From London, Blix and Tanne traveled to Paris. Tanne extravagantly invested in an entire new wardrobe made at Pacquin, before finally leaving for Denmark.

Blix did not stay long in Denmark, undoubtedly feeling

uneasy in the glare of mistrust and outright hostility from Tanne's family. He continued on to Sweden to face his own family. It was not until the following year, 1920, that he returned to Kenya.

Even if 1918 had been a fruitful year, expenditure never seemed to catch up with profit. Luck had not been on the Blixens' side during the previous six years. Ngong was wrong for coffee. The war had deprived them of making any real financial progress, since they had commandeered equipment, wagons, oxen, and labor. They had had to contend with two disastrous drought years, 1915 and 1918. Flax was planted at Uasin Gishu when the price was at its height; the price slumped to a record low shortly afterward. They lost their best ally in Ake Bursell, their manager, who was to become a most enterprising and successful farmer in his own right. The combination of bad luck, scant understanding of economics, and a taste for life's luxuries had reduced their dreams of enrichment to a reality of impoverishment. In the face of Blix's unsuccessful visit to Denmark, one gets the feeling that, on his return, he experienced the futility of it all and wished to sell out.

Until Tanne's return at the end of 1920, after having spent over a month in London and Paris on another buying spree, Blix led a wild social life. Olga Holmberg met Tanne and her brother Thomas on their arrival at Mombasa, regaled them with stories of the wild parties he had held in their house at Ngong, in the course of which a fair portion of Tanne's imported glass and crockery had come to grief. Blix had in fact

Berkeley Cole, one of Tanne's great favorites and a close friend of Denys Finch-Hatton. In the beginning of the war Cole gathered an equestrian force of 500 Somalis who went by the name of "Cole's Scouts." Cole died young and unmarried. He was extremely close to his mother—whom he adored—allegedly the reason why he never married.

ELDORET 168.
KITALE 209.
JINJA 376.
KAMPALA 429.
BUKOBA 656.
MBALE 325.
MONCALA 801.

carted half the furniture to the top of the Ngong Hills by ox-wagon to entertain friends before the backdrop of the setting sun.

During this period, Ben and Cockie Birkbeck came on a visit to Kenya, and Blix took them out on safari. Cockie rediscovered Blix's charm and enthusiasm, which had struck her on their first meeting in London the previous year. She fell in love. Their secret affair continued after the safari, and letters were passed, concealed in Emil Holmberg's gun barrels. Sometime later, Cockie felt it was time for the affair to end and said as much in a final billet-doux, stressing that their little adventure should at all costs remain a secret. The note was discovered by Olga Holmberg, who promptly showed it to Tanne.

Cockie soon learned her secret was out in the open. A few weeks later, she and Ben were lunching at the club with friends. Ben spotted Tanne and, unaware of his wife's dalliance, stopped by to chat. Tanne cut them both dead. When Cockie later related the incident, she said, "Cutting me dead proved she had no sense of humour. My God! Had it been me, I would have merely winked, 'Cockie *ma coquette*!' "

That year also saw the arrival from Sweden of two of Blix's close friends, Ingrid and Gillis Lindstrom, with their four small children. Gillis had arrived ahead of Ingrid with the idea of making a fortune in flax, leaving Ingrid to sell their estate and join him later. He made the mistake of attempting to buy a farm in Tanganyika from its German owner, but the British would not allow the sale of confiscated land to go through. Blix went with him to Tanganyika, but there was little he could do to help. The price of flax plummeted, so

It must have been difficult for Tanne to see almost everyone who had worked on "Karen Estate" become successful coffee farmers on their own land. Nils and Ette Fjastad, here with Emil Holmberg, right, were among them.

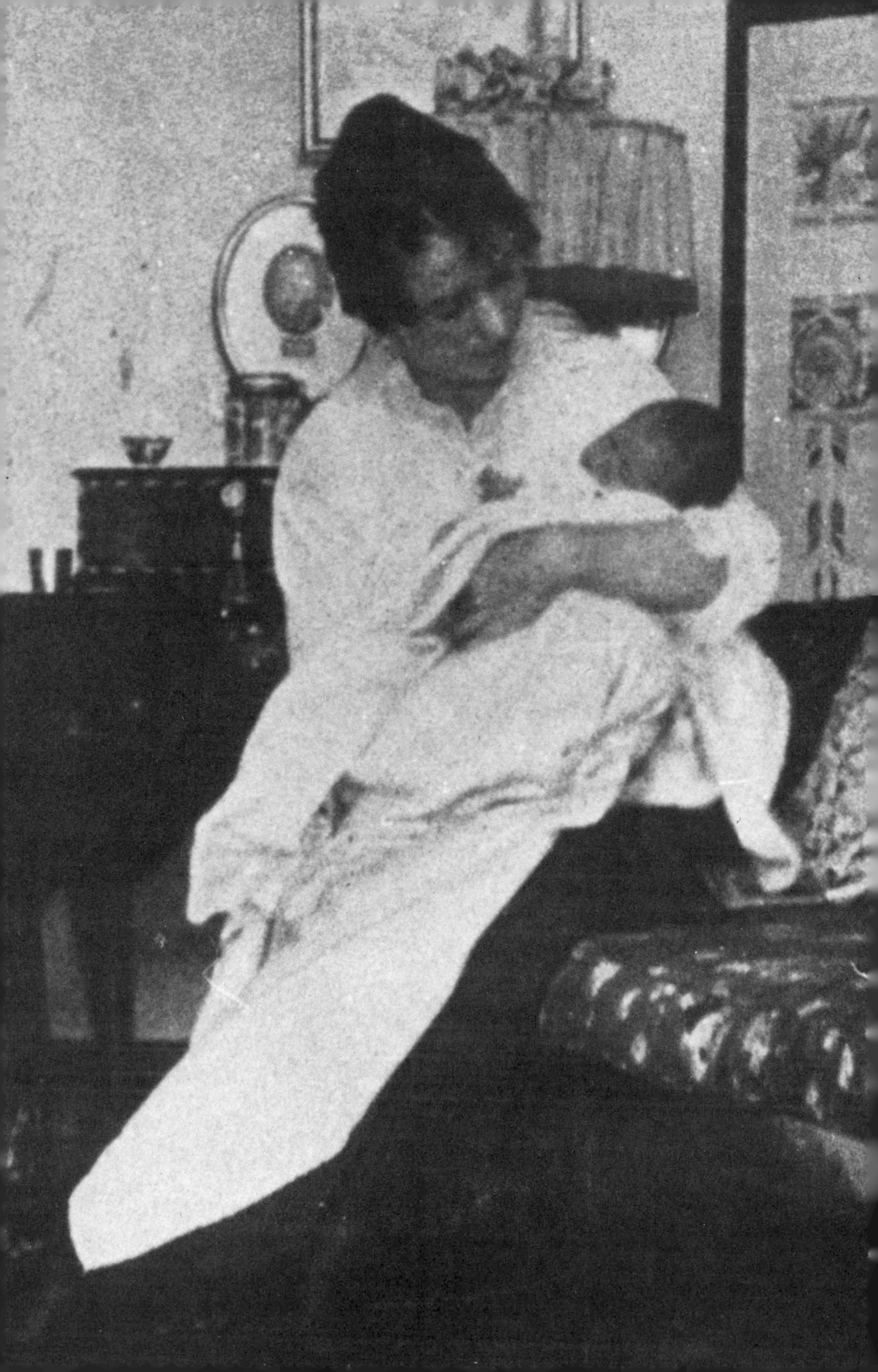

the two friends, at loose ends, took off on a hunting trip. Gillis cabled Ingrid not to bother to come out after all. Ingrid, by this time, was in Paris with her children and their governess, waiting to embark at Marseilles. To economize on their dwindling resources, she had moved to a cheaper hotel, so she never received the cable and arrived in Mombasa as planned. A farm was found for them at Njoro, which they bought from Geoffrey Buxton. The Birkbecks had also been interested in the farm, but Ben was unable to raise the cash.

In the spring of 1920, Aage Westenholz visited Kenya to see the situation first hand and to try to recoup some of the family's losses by selling the farm. Tanne wouldn't hear of it. Westenholz gave her one last, conditional chance: Blix was to be not only excluded from any say in the company but banned from the property altogether. If Tanne could not agree to this condition, the farm would be sold. Tanne agreed, and signed.

When she returned this damning statement to her uncle, she begged him not to disclose the contents of their agreement to anyone, either in Kenya or in Denmark. Although she must have found the decision incomprehensible and brutal, her fear of losing the farm and having to return to Denmark must have forced her hand. Her bad conscience about it was borne out by her reluctance to have others learn of it.

During this Westenholz trimming operation, the Holmbergs found themselves out of a job. Emil Holmberg bought land at Thika, which became one of the best coffee estates in the country.

Emil and Olga Holmberg were an oddly matched couple. Olga was a vivacious lady and not unfamiliar to the occasional flirtation. However, when he paid too much attention

Tanne with her godson Anders Holmberg, who later became one of Kenya's most prominent professional hunters and who now spends most of the year by Naivasha Lake in his godmother's old house.

to their English nanny, she banished him temporarily from the house under the pretext of recruiting more farm labor. Her humiliating discovery infuriated Emil, and his fury did not abate during his absence.

Krister Aschan (my father) and Ake Lindstrom (Gillis' nephew) were dining with Olga when Emil returned late one evening. He burst through the door, eyes blazing. Without a word, he drew his pistol, shot Olga through the chest, then took his own life. Miraculously, for he was a good shot, he missed killing Olga. Ake got her to a doctor and she subsequently lived to a grand old age, bolstered by champagne, taken on doctor's orders.

Meanwhile, my father was left to cope with the body of poor Emil. Unaccustomed to such nocturnal drama, he thought it best to get the advice of a fellow Swede, Sten Tham, who farmed on the same ridge. Laying Emil's inert form in the back of his boxbody car (a small truck with a roof over the bed but with open sides), he drove up to Tham's. Sten greeted him and asked him to dinner. Father declined, saying he had Emil in the back.

"Well, bring him in too. Hey, Emil, come on out and have something to eat," shouted Tham, then turned questioningly to my father. "What's he doing in the back, anyway?"

Father replied simply, "I'm afraid he's dead."

Blix had secured loans for himself against the farm, but he was a doomed man, hounded by creditors, with nowhere to go but the bush. He holed up for a time with the Lindstroms at Njoro. Gillis had straightened the access road so the approaching creditors could be seen from the house. The road ended in a quagmire in the rains, which deterred not only the unwanted but friends as well. For a time, Blix stayed with the governor, in whose house he was immune from prosecution. This in itself shows how popular he was.

Tanne's family now brought tremendous pressure to bear

on her to file for divorce, which she refused to do. Thomas, her brother, suggested to Aage Westenholz that they offer Blix an inducement to leave the country altogether, on payment of part of the sale price of the farm. Westenholz disagreed. He felt Blix would not be stupid enough to be bought out of the country.

By the time the farm was sold, at the height of the Depression in 1931, the family had poured in over £115,000 (about $500,000 in 1931). It was bought by Remy Martin, who purchased 5,300 acres for £10,000 on April Fool's Day. He offered Tanne the house and twenty acres. She turned it down, saying, "I would rather live on one acre in the Sahara desert than in the suburbs of Nairobi." Martin's first course of action was to pull up more than 600 acres of coffee they had so hopefully planted.

In spite of family adversity, Tanne remained loyal to Blix. She asked her mother to desist from pushing her into divorce, saying that matters between Blix and her were their own affair.

> I gave my word of honour that Bror would have nothing to do with the estate, and that's as far as I will go. If somebody asked me to join the Church of England because I had borrowed £200, I would refuse on the same principle.

But in 1921, they were separated. Tanne writes:

> As far as I am concerned, I can only say that I am unexpressively fond of Bror and it would be for me the greatest sorrow in the world to be divorced from him. I know very well that I by no means have been a good wife to him, but I do not think that there is anybody in the world who is as fond of him as I am.

Blix's debts were taken care of by friends. Cockie, worried that Blix might find himself imprisoned for debt, offered her pearls in settlement to one creditor, the owner of a Nairobi shop, the Dustpan. The creditor threw up his hands in horror

at the thought of her losing her precious necklace and simply wiped the slate clean, saying, "The Baron will hear no more of this little difficulty."

Shortly after the separation, Blix and Gillis Lindstrom were approached by the Swedish film industry to assist their photographer, a man named Olsson, on a wildlife documentary. The two men were to lead a secluded bush life for three months, which suited them both admirably.

In his book *Nyama,* Blix sums up those last eight years with the following scant description:

> The land was cleared. The coffee planted. The planter's pride and anticipation swelled in my chest. Summer went and Autumn came—the Autumn of 1914. The war. Chaos on the market, chaos in commerce. A beloved brother's death. The difficulties piled up. The plantation had to be sold—our home broken up. There I was empty handed in the bush. But, I still had my rifle!

Tanne was extremely devoted to her Irish Wolfhound, Dusk, who unfortunately died when left in the care of a good friend.

He could outshoot, outwalk and outdrink anyone. He could also out-charm the ladies, and although he was my mother's cousin my father never dared let my mother meet Blix.

—ANTHONY DYER

Five

The Professional Hunter: 1922–1928

ND SO BLIX BEGAN his professional hunting career.

Close to the Murchison Falls Game Reserve in Uganda, the elephants were spilling out onto neighboring native cultivations, causing havoc and leaving destruction in their wake. The game department deemed it necessary to contain the herds through culling. Blix volunteered and was accepted for the job. He hired an additional two porters to carry his bed, blankets, ammunition, and the minimum rations of salt, tea, sugar, rice, and flour. He and his two gunbearers pitched their camp at Masindi.

Blix was immediately taken with the area. While resting under the tree where Samuel Baker had camped in 1864, he would muse at its past and chequered history. He hunted along the same trails that Baker and his wife had followed in their quest for the source of the Nile, and he looked to the hills south of Masindi from whose summit Baker had first seen Lake Albert. Little did he suspect that the old missionary, Livingstone, believed to be missing, was in fact encamped a short distance away at Kasenyi.

Kabarega of Bunyoro, the warrior king, had ruled the region for more than twenty years, from 1876 to 1899, with a cruel and cunning hand. None of the earlier explorers—Baker, Gordon, Stanley, and Lugard among them—had succeeded in diminishing his power. He was feared by all who met him. In 1899, when the English finally drove him out, he joined forces with his old archenemy Mwanga, who ruled a small kingdom on the shores of Lake Victoria. There, in the vast papyrus swamps, the English became engaged in a lengthy struggle with the two kings. Eventually, a native was bribed to disclose the enemy's whereabouts, and during the last battle, Mwanga surrendered. Kabarega, his spear-throwing arm blown off, his faithful lying dead around him, fought courageously until one of his chieftains held him down to prevent him from continuing battle. While Mwanga bemoaned his fate, Kabarega looked out across the low, marshy country and said deprecatingly, "What are you wailing for? If I were king of this rotten country, I would thank the English for throwing me out." Kabarega was never again to see his beloved mountains for he and Mwanga were exiled to the Seychelles, where he died in 1923. But he was still alive when Blix was resting under that tree.

In his guise as deliverer from the new elephant plague, Blix's arrival was greeted with great joy. He wandered from village to village, assessing the damage and listening patiently to the villagers' complaints. Quite a few elephant fell before his rifle, and wherever he went feasts and dances were laid on in his honor.

> Fires were lit, the drums came out and soon the night vibrated with the monotonous, but curiously inspiring, beat. Young girls with figures like Venus, a mass of swaying loins. In the fluttering light of the fires their bodies shone like bronze through a veil of dust.

It is evident from Blix's notes covering this period that here, at last, he had found his niche. Taking a few days' break, he moved camp to below the Murchison Falls. "The spectacular panorama defies description and can only be set to music or painted," he wrote. Here is one of the places in Africa where the setting most resembles the image of the Garden of Eden. Colors of the rainbow shimmer in the fall's fine spray. Magnificent fish eagles soar over its heights. Cormorants, stilts, and Jacanas strut and wade between banks of crocodiles lying immobile as if touched by magic, petrified in their stillness. Wallowing hippo peer lazily above the water with arched brow. A herd of elephant and young calves sport in the shallower reaches, mindless of approaching gazelles, ears flickering, eye and body alert to danger.

During his time spent on elephant control, Blix recounted the following incident:

> Confined to camp one wet day two men from a nearby village came to tell me that a man had been killed by elephant while gathering honey, and asked if I would come at once to shoot it. We set off for the village to find everyone running about like giddy geese. The men brandished sharpened spears while women seated on small stools ululated like dogs at full moon. They were hired mourners brought in to wail for days on end. It was a morbid scene but induced a suitably funereal mood. Not far from the village, vultures circled over the spot where the man had been killed. We set off accompanied by my gun-bearer, Juma, my .600 double-barrel rifle,* and a couple of men to show the way. Before reaching the dead man we came across two of his companions perched high in the trees, too afraid to come down. From their babbled description we learned that the men had been wandering along the path looking for bees when the elephant charged without warning, scattering the honey hunters in every direction. Before their hapless friend could take cover, the elephant had

*Blix's favorite elephant gun was .505 Gibb, which took three cartridges in the magazine and one in the breach. For other big game he used a .416 Rigby and a .256 Mannlicher for smaller game. Asked once what rifle he would prefer if only given the choice of one as an all-around gun, his choice was the .318 Westley & Richards.

A professional hunter must have a heavy-, medium-, and a light-gauge rifle at his disposal, as well as a shotgun. Gauge varies according to the hunter's personal preference. Heavy gauge might range from between 15 to 11 millimeters, medium from 11 to 9 mm., and light from 8. to 6.5 mm.

reached out, encircled his trunk about the man's waist, and dashing him repeatedly against the tree, speared him again and again as 'if he had been a piece of dough.' The elephant finally knelt on him, crushing every bone in his body. We soon found the dead man, mutilated beyond recognition. His face alone remained intact and I shall never forget the expression of indescribable fear that marked his features. The ground around him was covered in blood. The still shaking trees and wild trumpeting heralded the elephant's proximity. Picking up the tracks from the melee of crushed vegetation and furrowed ground I deduced from their small size that she must be a cow elephant. Half an hour later we came across some fresh steaming dung and realised we must be close. The forest was thick with heavy undergrowth. There was no sound. Juma was ahead of me examining every bush and blade of grass. As we came out onto a small clearing I accidentally stepped on a twig. The sharp snap was immediately followed by a deafening trumpet blast and the elephant was upon us. I shot and jumped out of her way to the right, Juma to the left. The bullet appeared to have no impact and she charged, trunk levelled at Juma. I gave her the second barrel and reloaded. Suddenly within ten yards Juma sprinted past me with the mad cow close on his heels. This time I brained her. She fell trunk outstretched and all four legs pointing backwards six paces from the last of her tracks so she must have been going flat out.

Juma then reappeared and said with a wide grin, "I thought I'd better lead her past you." Calm, brave, honest old Juma! What a man.

The tusks were long and narrow, the left one still covered in skin and dried blood, and in the creases of her knees bits of flesh remained embedded. I kept the blooded tusks as a memory to Juma's bravery when in the face of death he deliberately led her past me.

After another month of control work, Blix was satisfied that he had persuaded the elephants to return within the reserve boundaries. In the process he had collected a fair amount of ivory, adding a further £500 (about $2,270 at the time) to his contract from the half-share to which he was entitled.

Before his return to Kenya, Blix hired a motor boat to visit a small, uninhabited island on Lake Victoria which he had set his heart on somehow acquiring. This paradise—a half-moon stretch of about 100 acres, bordered with a lagoon etched in

(Following page) *Blix with a felled water buffalo.*

chalk-white sand—was purchased with the help of a friend for £10 (about $45) a year on a ninety-year lease. The northern end was thickly forested with trees hung with liana and lichen, and Blix entertained the idea of releasing monkeys and chimpanzees there. At the center of the island he envisioned building his future house, on a glade overlooking the small stream that ran below the cliff.

Blix wrote of the island:

> In the forest there was an abundance of bird life—green and grey parrots, weaver and sun birds. Hornbills flew with heavy wing above the treetops and in the thicker foliage I saw glimpses of a Turaco's flashing purple-red wings. Ducks bobbed gently in the bay and two fish eagles were perched on a dry overhang. Their heads shone white against the blue-black sky and their handsome brown attire reflected the sun's rays. Hippos grazed the glades; their tracks cutting a wide swathe through the grass. We also saw evidence of waterbuck and sitatunga beside the stream. They must have swum across from the mainland.

Blix's return to Nairobi was short-lived, with high hedonistic living taking its toll on his recently acquired fortune. He was, however, eager to return, and headed northwest once again. This time he intended to travel further west into the Belgian Congo.

At Butiaba, on the eastern shores of Lake Albert, he stopped briefly to shoot buffalo, since an Asian trader at Masindi had promised good money for the hides. Here, again, Blix is preoccupied with this as yet unexploited region's past and future and the contradictions surrounding the discovery of the Nile source:

> Lake Victoria is one of the Nile's great reservoirs. Most of its waters originate from the Semliki River that drains the Ruwenzori Mountains whose snow masses and prolific rain provide a constant flow, swollen by streams emanating from the highlands between Kasenyi and Mahegi. The Nile flows

> out of the northern end of the lake where it tapers into a funnel, and joins the Victoria Nile further north. Its source deluded many an explorer although Ptolemy came close when he wrote of two lakes and the Mountains of the Moon being the 'mothers of the Nile'. Speke was the first white man to see Lake Victoria in 1861, and Baker the first to see Lake Albert three years later.
>
> It was therefore with a deep sense of awe that I first trod those paths. Everything was seemingly unchanged and was as it had probably always been for thousands of years—the only difference being the one road and a few modern boats on the lake.
>
> Unchanged too are the habits and traditions of the people. They build the same huts and eat the same food. Elephant, hippo, and buffalo tread the same paths, crocodile fish the same waters, undisturbed now as then. Will a future generation's 'civilising' influence destroy all this? Will the white man conquer the black, or vice versa? Will science overcome disease or modernisation exploit these vast, rich regions?
>
> Its lakes [are] rich in fish and millions of fertile acres could sustain coffee, tea, maize, sisal and cattle—more than enough to support an undeveloped world. It was here that Emin Pasha and his troops found themselves cut off from Egypt due to General Gordon's defeat in the Sudan, and were forced to establish a self-supporting state. When Stanley finally arrived in 1887 having crossed the Congo's primeval forests to relieve them, Emin Pasha refused to leave. Oh! how well I understand him!

Blix now crossed into the Belgian Congo and the Ituri Forest, hoping to catch a glimpse of the rare okapi, a strange-looking animal with a short, compact body and sloping back. Its general color is dark chestnut, with creamy white legs conspicuously striped in black. Nocturnal, the okapi lives in dense rain forest and is a wary and elusive creature. Blix set up his base camp by the River Nepoko, west of the Ituri forest, among a small tribe of pygmies, the Wambuti, the original dwellers of the area. His curiosity and natural inclination to discover more about his surroundings and its inhabitants brought him into closer contact with the tribe, from whom he learned a great deal. He writes of the white man's limitations in dealing with this new foreign and hostile habitat:

> The white man cannot hope to cover the rugged terrain mile after mile in silence, nor swing across rivers on lianas, or steal honey from wild bees, catch parrot chicks high in the trees, gather fruit from the oil palm ninety feet up. He knows little of the barks and roots used for dyes and cooking.

With the little Wambuti's help, Blix saw okapi on seven different occasions. He had also purchased five elephant licenses and sent Wambuti scouts in every direction. Word came that there were fresh tracks not far from camp. Like a pointer, the Wambuti scout advanced ahead with a light, razor-sharp throwing spear, rigidly lifting each stork-like leg in turn. When Blix caught a glimpse of the tusks, he saw they were miserably small. He motioned negatively to his friend, who was not so easily put off and made it clear that he would pursue the quarry himself.

> The Wambuti do not usually kill elephant with a throwing spear but rather with a wide, short thrusting spear which requires great skill and bravery. The Wambuti advanced slowly, arm raised, muscles taut as steel. I was behind and had never been so close to an unwounded elephant. My eyes were fixed to the spot where I would shoot. I sensed, rather than saw, how the little dwarf leaned back, bringing his left arm up for balance while his spear and right arm arched out in one swift movement, the spear cutting the air straight for

During his first expedition to the Belgian Congo, Blix was accompanied by a band of pygmies who were a source of great help and joy to him. The little girl is Suleima who nursed him during his time of serious illness.

the elephant's heart. As it struck, the elephant lifted his head and turned towards us. My bullet broke his neck. I will never forget the moment. The little man showed no particular joy or surprise, just a dignified pride. He cut off the tail as a token of his success and prowess as a hunter.

I have witnessed the voraciousness of vultures but nothing to compare with that of those forty pygmies, men and women, in the way they tackled the carcass, dipping their knives and spear blades deep into the meat. There followed that evening a strange feast. The utter primitiveness was made all the more real by the knowledge that few white men could have witnessed or disturbed this little atavistic group. The drums beat out a monotonous rattle and the village vibrated to the pounding of feet. Suddenly into the circle of dancers leaped the little hunter, his greased body shining red in the firelight, to take his place of honour at the centre, spear and elephant's tail held high. In a sea of waving spears the village pantomine commenced—the hunt, fallen elephant, division of spoils—and the forest echoed to the sounds of music and laughter. At the peak of the dance's frenetic height the child figure of a young girl materialised into the arms of the little elephant hunter and bodies surrendered themselves to wild abandonment.

The tangible atmosphere of those regressive rites will forever remain vivid. To this day I can still feel the ground quiver under their tiny feet.

Blix collected his five elephant and, pleased with the results, applied for additional licenses in an adjoining area.

His small group had now turned into a safari caravan with the addition of two local girls for Juma and Abedi, the cook, and a handful of servants. There were also fifty porters hired to carry ivory, cloth, food, and equipment. Blix befriended a young chimpanzee and a parrot, which he taught to say "Go to Hell!" in several languages. Wherever they went, they were greeted as heroes dispensing free meat. In return, the chiefs offered up young girls and the pick of the

Sometimes the terrain in which Blix hunted during these years could only be negotiated on foot. Equipment, supplies, and ammunition had to be carried by bearers hired for the occasion.

elephant within their boundaries. Blix refused neither.

While they were still encamped in the Ituri Forest, the rains broke, slowing the pace as the column of porters slid and fell beneath the weight of heavy burdens. Rafts had to be built to ford flooded rivers. Food supplies became dangerously scarce, with an expected ten-day journey ahead to the next village. On the fourth day, one of the porters was taken ill. Blix suspected and treated him for pneumonia, but he died in the night. At dawn the following day he was buried, according to custom, seated in an upright position, surrounded by all he possessed. Two days later, another man was similarly buried, and Blix sent two runners ahead to get food. That evening, while Blix himself was out hunting for camp meat, he too began to feel the onslaught of fever. His temperature rose rapidly, and by nightfall he was unconscious. Lying delirious for several days, he had little recollection of time passing. On waking, he remembers Suleima, Abedi's girlfriend, holding his hand and looking down at him with tear-filled eyes. This prompted him to write,

> Why is it that a woman, regardless of colour, is of so much more solace to a man in distress? Why do we feel such comfort when death is near? How can she alone understand and know so well our needs?

The two runners returned a week later from the village with food, and Blix slowly regained his strength. Reports arrived daily of huge elephants roaming the plains. Blix, himself too weak to move, sent Juma to investigate the rumors. On his return two weeks later, it was evident that these had been well founded and that indeed the tusks were "as thick as my thigh." Blix was moved on a stretcher and reached the village that had so long awaited them. It took them six days to reach it, instead of the expected three. On his arrival, he was given a freshly made hut and a nourishing meal and fell happily to sleep under the comforting gaze of Suleima.

Juma came to report a couple of days later that a big bull elephant had been seen less than an hour away. "If you are too tired to shoot, at least come and have a look at it," he urged. The chief had placed his ceremonial sedan-chair and eight porters at Blix's disposal. His spirit was willing, if not his body, and he felt he owed his hosts a debt. He did feel it rather demeaning to be carried to a hunt, but no one else seemed to find the situation in any way unusual, as it had always been the way chiefs and Belgian professional hunters pursued the sport.

The porters put the chair down 500 yards from the bull

and, much to Blix's surprise, after being laid up for two long months, he managed to walk the rest of the way. The elephant, bearing tusks of over ninety pounds, was shot where he stood. It seemed to Juma, Abedi, and camp followers that the string of recent bad luck had finally been broken.

On the mend, Blix wrote to a friend:

> When I last wrote to you I was, I believe, quite weak. However, I am now fit again and can once more walk the feet off my gun bearers. I feel the sun is brighter, the birds more beautiful, and my blood runs thicker. Sorrows and troubles no longer seem insuperable. We have shot five elephant—not bad for our little party of men. Juma is in splendid form. He can now unashamedly conduct his own business with the locals, extracting tobacco and beer (strong and nourishing—a local brew from Matma seed and bark) for supplies of fresh meat. He has been heard on more than one occasion to insinuate, as he oversees the procession of baskets of meat borne on the backs of the Chief's copper-coloured harem, that 'Beautiful girls have always been my weakness.'
>
> Our camp lacks for nothing. Girls with supple back and slender neck bear jars of beer, bananas, chickens and eggs, rice and oil. Peace and happiness dominate our existence. The young dance and sing while the elders sit and talk. We talk about days gone by. So much has changed in the last fifty years with 'civilisation' encroaching on the old ways. Once the elders have gained the white man's confidence they open up their hearts and what they have to say is fascinating. Theirs is a wisdom and common sense passed down by word of mouth from generation to generation and cannot be learned from books.
>
> One evening with the beer freely flowing the conversation took a turn which gave me cause for concern and left me feeling doubtful as to their future. The advent of missionaries had brought conflicting teachings—Catholic and Lutheran faiths. They were bewildered and confused. Tribal warfare had been forbidden and while the resulting peace allowed them

easy access across tribal frontiers to trade, the Chief turned to me accusingly, and said, 'You, my white friend, do not always live as you preach. You wage war on each other while forbidding us this our ancient tradition!' Who was I to argue?

Having never seen a stone building, the Wambuti warriors were wide-eyed with amazement on first reaching Beni, a small enclave of permanent buildings nestling at the foothills of the Ruwenzoris, north of Lake Edward. Blix based himself here at a little Italian-run hotel, where he met the only other permanent resident, a Belgian vet and old elephant hand. The Belgian loaned his two elephant trackers, who teamed up with Blix's loyal followers to establish an intelligence network. Reports from nearby villages began filtering in most evenings, but when followed up, they gave negative results. The ivory was either too small or the elephant had just pushed off. Blix was in no hurry, and daily excursions into the forest totally absorbed him.

The forest is a stark picture of contrasts. Oil palms weave their slender forms between tall mahogany. Rough-barked teak stand densely erect, their branches sprung like the spokes of an umbrella—hence its Swahili name, "Mwivuli." The sight of a leopard sunning itself on a fallen tree barely comes into focus against the filtered rays of dappled light, which form a myriad of shape and color on the forest floor. The murmur of running water masked all sound, and while Blix stood transfixed, his gunbearer handed him a rifle. Although sorely tempted, he felt to loose off a bullet then would be like "farting in church!"

Sightseeing aside, Blix could no longer ignore reports of big ivory centered on the area around the Okiti Mountain, a couple of days walk from Beni. With dawn a pale glimmer to the east and the dew heavy underfoot, the party set off. Creamy white lilies had proceeded the rains, and the trees were festooned with overhanging orchids. Crystal-clear

Everyone is up early and leaves the camp before sunrise. If the purpose is hunting, they're gone most of the day and return only after nightfall. On a photo safari the routine is somewhat different: Early call to tea or coffee; leave camp before the sun is up; back around 11 A.M. for a hardy English breakfast of fruit, egg and bacon, freshly baked bread, and other delicacies; relaxation in and around the camp until around 3 P.M., when a light lunch is served (salad, cheese and fruit, for instance), and later out again to return to camp after dark. Dinner is served by candelight and usually consists of three courses served with two kinds of wine.

streams ran blindly beneath overhanging palms and ferns. Parrots whistled shrilly overhead, and the forest echoed to the sweet song of the oriole. Blix felt elated and wondered how the peculiarities of the Marua people could ever have been practiced among such beautiful surroundings. This small tribe from the southern end of Kivu district had been ruled up until the turn of the century by a succession of despotic kings, each one more barbaric than the last. King Kasongo, believed to possess magical powers, claimed he did not need to eat or drink in order to survive, but did so purely in pursuit of pleasure. He also claimed the right to take any woman throughout the kingdom for his personal gratification, where and whenever he pleased. Like Cleopatra warming her feet on the backs of slaves, Kasongo would sit or recline and even walk on female slaves, wallowing in the soft folds of warm flesh. In death he lay cocooned in a pyre of slowly suffocating living forms, all in a pit at the bottom of a diverted stream-bed. Once the mass of bodies had been covered over with soil, the blood of an equal number of male slaves would be poured over the grave before the stream could resume its course.

In a letter to a friend, Blix wrote:

> Unburdened of heavy loads we set off at a fast pace stopping at four as night falls early in the forest. With the loads lined up everybody helped to make a clearing. This has to be chosen with care to avoid being knocked out by a falling branch while asleep. There was no need for tentage as the forest provided ample shelter. Cut saplings were staked out supporting broad-leafed roofs. With water close at hand nothing more was required. The fires lit, the Wambuti wandered off in search of honey. Nobody seemed tired that night, least of all Bao, the little Wambuti girl who had followed us all the way from the Nepoko River. Seated around the campfire after a good meal of chicken curry, coffee and brandy, Bao entertained us on the lute accompanied by her

equally diminutive friend on his bamboo flute. There was a warm spirit of friendship and infinite peace among the small gathering. It felt good to be alive.

Around midnight on the second evening, the peace was shattered by an invasion of safari ants. Feared throughout Africa by man and beast alike, these shiny black insects move in one vast column—a foot abreast—spearheaded by soldier ants, with workers and female ants bringing up the rear, carrying food and eggs. They relentlessly attack and destroy anything that has the misfortune to find itself in the way, and they will regroup farther on. Their vise-like pincers are impossible to pry off and remain embedded in flesh long after the body has been detached. It took Blix and his men the entire night to fight off this marauding pack. But in spite of their lack of sleep, the following morning they picked up sizeable bull tracks. By nightfall Blix had collected two magnificent trophies.

During this period, Blix continued his courtship of Cockie by letter. She was still married to Birkbeck, who was then in England raising money to buy a farm in Kenya.

Before leaving for the Congo, Blix had arranged for a friend, Jeff Manley, to act as his safari agent. Manley had good contacts abroad, and Blix was soon taking out his first hunting clients professionally.

One of his first was Sir Charles Markham, whose coalmining interest in the north of England enabled him to indulge in the new sport of big game hunting. A giant of a man, Markham stood six and a half feet tall. He towered over his young wife, Glady, whose doll-like appearance belied a strong, discerning temperament.

The Markhams and their white hunter traveled by train to Kampala in Uganda, where Blix's Model T Ford was loaded with light camping equipment and stores. From there they traveled by road to Lake Albert to spend a few relaxed days fishing, before heading north to hunt big ivory along the Nile River. The district officer, forewarned of the visit, had organized extra porters—the sight of fifty naked men standing to attention was an impressive sight.

The area had been part of the Lado Enclave, a vast region stretching from Lake Albert in the south, the Sudan to the north, and bordered west and east by the Congo and Upper Nile. It had been leased to King Leopold II for his life, plus six months. The half-year extension was added to give Belgian officials time to pack up and leave. Upon Leopold's death, the Belgians abandoned the region sooner than expected, leaving the area lawless. Into this "no-man's land" poured a motley assortment of men from all walks of life, who had been fired by tales of enrichment: contractors, hotel keepers, farmers, soldiers, government employees, and a handful of bona fide hunters. Each man was a law unto himself in a country long accustomed to the atrocities wrought by a foreign power blinded by greed. Game was haphazardly shot and left wounded, and the inhabitants, evening out the score for past misdeeds, were suspicious and treacherous. Many a hunting neophyte was killed by elephant. Quite a few did make a fortune by dint of courage and sacrifice, and one or two by sheer luck.

One, an eccentric English itinerant, entered this scene of desperados fresh-faced and fashionably dressed, but with neither gun nor money. He traveled from village to village where he eked out a living at the mercy of local hospitality. The African people felt he must be under the protection of some divine being and hence perfectly harmless. When others asked what he thought he was doing there, he simply shrugged and replied, "Waiting for something to happen." Nothing did. Half starved, his fashionable clothes now in shreds, he staggered into a Belgian outpost. The Belgians took pity on him. They fed him, dressed him in one of their uniforms, and finally, impatient to be rid of the responsibility, pointed him homeward. Left on the Nile shore, the Belgian escort barely out of sight, he stumbled on an Asian poacher preparing to boat his ill-gotten gains across the river. The poacher, frightened by the sight of uniform, fled with his porters across the river, leaving behind his precious hoard of ivory. Undaunted, the Englishman wasted no time in procuring other porters with his new-found badge of office and ferried the load across the river. Selling it on the other side for a handsome profit, he happily returned to England a rich man.

When Blix and Sir Charles Markham arrived at rhino camp, law and order had once again been restored. The area, now part of the Ugandan protectorate, was administered by the British. Elephants could be shot only by license.

Blix learned that there were elephant less than five miles from camp. In the predawn stillness, the party made ready to leave. Porters ferried hampers of food and drink, rations, and bedding in the event they should find themselves benighted. It was late afternoon before they caught up with the elephant, a herd of between 400 and 500. Glady Markham was beginning to feel the heat, so Blix called a halt, sending trackers ahead to scout for the big bulls.

On their return, Blix led the advance, skirting the forest to keep downwind of two bulls, who, unaware of the intruders, stood listlessly in the shade of a tree, heads bowed, ears lazily flapping. An anthill lay between hunter and quarry, toward which Blix led them. Like some prehistoric reptile, the line moved cautiously. No one dared to make the slightest sound.

Glady Markham was first to shoot. As she raised the gun, the smaller of the two bulls suddenly ambled out in front of her sights. Silently expelling the last few seconds of pent-up emotion, she lowered the gun and looked inquiringly at Blix. Minutes of agonizing waiting passed, sweated out while flies buzzed around with impunity. No one dared to move a hand in retaliation. Finally, the elephant moved on and she was able to get a clean shot off. With mixed feelings of elation and sadness, Glady had successfully claimed her first elephant. Sir Charles shot the second, its tusks slightly smaller than the first. While based at rhino camp, they also collected rhino, lion, cob, and waterbuck.

From there they traveled north again, to Arua and up as far as the Sudan border. By the Kai River they spotted a magnificent herd of Lord Derby's eland. These are the largest of the African antelopes. They carry immense, spiral horns, and a big bull will weigh over 1,500 pounds. White rhino were also in abundance. Unlike the black rhino, they are more cow-like in temperament. Out alone one afternoon, Blix came across a bull rhino's track that struck him as odd, for it was preceded by a deep zigzag groove. Intrigued by this abnormal imprint, he followed it up; a few hours later he came upon the sleeping giant. His head was bowed by the weight of two colossal horns, the lower one reached the ground in a downward sweep. Close by, in a wallow, Blix measured the horn from the print left in the mud. It measured out at forty-two and a half inches.

Closeted together for weeks at a time, hunter and client can develop a very special relationship. The two share a love of adventure, foremost, and have the time to get to know each other well. Blix and Markham got on extremely well from the start, making a friendship that was to last a lifetime. Markham suggested they do another trip of a very different nature, crossing Africa from east to west on a compass bearing.

"You do realize there are no roads," said Blix.

"We'll make our own."

Glady Markham became pregnant, however, and the trip was postponed indefinitely.

Their next hunting trip, that same year, took them to the Congo. They set out from Mahegi, west of Lake Albert's

A hunting or photo safari (then as now) demands detailed preparation if everything is to proceed smoothly. The supplies, which are both extensive and bulky, might include: mess tent, sleeping tent, toilet tent, shower tent, kitchen tent, beds, mattresses, bedding, table, chairs, kitchenware, canteens, gasoline, refrigerator, and fresh water. Together with the participants this is transported on a large four-wheel-drive truck. Perishables, fruit, mail—and perhaps the Sunday news—are flown in to the camp at least once a week.

northern end, with a cavalcade of porters. After the first night, half the porters had disappeared. Blix was wondering how he was going to make up the difference when he discovered they were camped in King Julu's territory. King Julu was one of the few men alive who had fought against the warrior king Kabarega, and Blix was eager to make his acquaintance. Blix sent word to invite the old man to camp that evening. To everyone's surprise, King Julu arrived that afternoon. They talked long into the night. Unfortunately, there is no record of their conversation. However, Blix's royal connection seemed to have produced the necessary pull, and porters arrived the following morning by the score.

They now passed through the Gumbari district, renowned for its cannibalistic tribes. Paying his respects to the residing chief, Blix gently led the conversation around to the subject of human flesh. He asked the old man which parts he considered the most delectable. The chief was not about to be drawn out. While admitting that such barbaric habits had probably belonged to the past, he said he himself was not aware of the practice. Blix must have looked incredulous, for the old man said, "You are here to shoot elephant. At the end of the day you eat chicken. Your men eat the meat. At the end of a day's battle my men eat the spoils while I, like you, eat chicken." He let his words sink in for a moment, then his face cracked into a wide smile, lighting up a thousand wrinkles. He added, "The best part is actually the one you're sitting on!"

At the end of the last century, tribal prisoners would be publicly auctioned. Prospective buyers chalked down choice pieces, so the life expectancy of the hapless victim was measured by the time it took to mark off his "joints" in their entirety. During the Congo debacle in 1960–1963, a friend of mine witnessed the sale of shrunken hands in a marketplace. He was not certain whether they belonged to man or monkey.

Blix's theory was that cannibalism was so widespread in the Congo due to the forest's comparative scarcity of game. Weapons were primitive, and the lack of grazing inconducive to keeping livestock. Another theory is that game meat brought disease. Today, in parts of southern Sudan, it is still believed that bongo meat causes venereal disease.

The hunting party then worked its way down to Beni and, eventually, Lake Kivu, a land of gently rolling hills interspersed with tongues of forest and streams. They arrived at the little town of Goma, reflected in the lake's northern end and surrounded by forested craters to the east and the Ruwenzori mountains to the north. Its perfect climate and idyllic setting prompted Markham to dream of creating a luxury health resort that would empty the beaches of Cannes and Biarritz and shut down the casinos of Monte Carlo and Palm Beach. In 1962, I was based at Bukava on Kivu's southern shore for six months with the dubious honor of serving the United Nations forces. I therefore share Markham's view of Kivu, but not the idea of sharing it with all of Europe's sun worshippers.

During their stay at Goma, they witnessed the spectacular sight of an erupting volcano. Blix had spotted the arrival of an aeroplane that morning from Nairobi and persuaded the pilot to take them up for a closer look. "The lava, like molten rivers of iron ore emerging from a gigantic furnace slowly made its way down the slopes. Trees, set alight, toppled over like matchsticks. A heavy pall of smoke and gas lay over the mass." Shortly after this entertaining display, Blix and Markham, their quota fulfilled, returned to Nairobi.

Another client who was to become a close friend was also an Englishman, Major Richard Cooper, simply known as "Dick." Cooper arrived with the novel idea that hunting with a bow and arrow would be far more sporting than hunting with a gun. Blix exerted great tact in persuading him to the contrary. Cooper wished to hunt for lion. For this hunt,

Blix journeyed south to Tanganyika and the areas around and beyond Lake Manyara.

Lion are either tracked up, baited, flushed, or "galloped" on horses in open country. The latter practice, discontinued by 1914, involves the method of "talley-ho-ing" the lion, who eventually stands his ground. At that point, the hunter dismounts to shoot, hoping like hell his aim is true and his horse doesn't bolt. This required exceptional courage. Blix's preferred tactic was to flush the lion out, much as he did with hares and rabbits, as a boy at Nasbyholm. Beaters would drive the lion out of thick bush or swamp, where they tended to lie up in the heat of the day, toward the hunter. In this way, a large black-maned lion was driven toward Cooper, who shot but only wounded it. The lion emitted a single deep groan and disappeared into the thicket.

It is an unwritten law that a hunter never leaves a wounded animal, no matter how dangerous the circumstances. It takes a great deal of courage, however, to walk in blind after a wounded lion. The lion's acute senses of survival are highly tuned, especially when wounded. He hears and senses your every move without revealing his position until he is well within striking distance.

Blix instructed his assistant hunter, Neil, a young Boer, to climb the nearest acacia and locate the lion's position. When he was barely halfway up, the lion sprang toward Blix and to within inches of Neil's dangling feet. Blix's first shot temporarily arrested the lion, but spurred on by adrenaline, the lion kept coming. The second shot finally dropped him. Wryly observing the dead lion at his feet, Blix turned to Cooper and said, "Still want to try your bow and arrow?"

The areas between the Mbulu plateau and the Essimingor Hills were to become Blix's favorite hunting ground. Cooper was also taken by its beauty, and he eventually bought a farm nearby at Babati, south of the Ngorongoro Crater and immediately west of today's Tarangire National Park.

Leaving the lions once again at peace, the party traveled north to Engaruka and Ol Donyo Lengai ("mountain of God" in Maasai). This African paradise, teeming with game, had been earmarked before World War I for development by German settler-farmers. After the Versailles treaty, the British returned the land to the Maasai.

Just south of Ol Donyo Lengai lies Ngorongoro Crater, still one of the most spectacular game haunts in Africa. It is also one of the biggest craters in the world. It measures more than nine miles across, 2,500 feet deep, and covers 100 square miles. Open, grassy plains dotted with fresh and brackish lakes and acacia woodland adorn its base, while its rim is thickly forested. In those days, the crater and its surrounding hills were privately owned by Sir Charles Ross, an ardent conservationist. Laying rifles aside, Blix and Cooper spent a delightful week behind the camera, obtaining some unique footage.

From Ngorongoro, the two friends continued southeast across the Yaida Valley to the shores of Lake Eyasi. At its southern end lies a swamp surrounded by steep cliffs, among which lived a small tribe related to the pygmy bushmen, the Wadiki-Diki. The name probably derived along with the small gazelle, the dik-dik. The tribe moved with and lived on the game. They occupied basic, temporary dwellings that could easily be moved and set down again, in keeping with their migratory habits. Blix made friends with them, and they were always keen to share their knowledge of game and game movements with him.

On their return to Nairobi, Blix learned that Cockie had left for England. He was disappointed, but the social whirl soon distracted him. At a party, he met a young Swedish girl who also happened to be staying at the Norfolk Hotel. As a habitué, he was able to switch rooms to one adjoining hers. However, a sudden bout of pneumonia prevented him from forming any sort of liaison; his nights were spent sitting bolt

Blix, in the second position, guiding a party in the bush.

upright, valiantly attempting to supress his coughing fits to avoid disturbing the young woman's sleep.

While tying up loose safari ends in Nairobi, Blix would base himself at the Norfolk, from where he would reach out to old friends, including his former wife Tanne. Although he was unable to help her financially in the running of the farm, she continued to depend on him for support, and she never called on him in vain.

On a visit to the Lindstroms at Njoro in 1923, he arrived to find a family in contention. Ingrid's younger sister, Ette De Mare, had been invited by the handsome Swede, Nils

Fjastad, to a dance in Nairobi but had no means of getting there; the Lindstroms' ancient car was too valuable to risk on pleasure jaunts. Although tired out after a day's journey, Blix made the six-hour drive back to Nairobi, getting her there just in time for the party.

While Ette was out in Kenya, she stayed with Tanne on the farm at Ngong. "It was all very grand," recalls Ette, "the place milling with servants carrying in morning tea on silver trays. The table was always laid as if for a dinner party with serried ranks of glasses which, I must confess, were rarely filled."

On her second visit in 1925, now engaged to be married to Nils Fjastad, she traveled out on the boat from Rotterdam with Tanne and her Danish wolfhounds. During one of the boat's rougher passages, Ette confided her fear to Tanne, "I hope we're not going down."

"I wouldn't mind," was all Tanne replied.

In 1923, Blix had written to Tanne from the Congo to tell her that he could help her to get the loan she needed to buy out the Danish shareholders. One can only presume he had approached the Markhams, for Tanne then wrote to her brother to say she had had a visit from one of Blix's clients, a lady, proposing financial help through the lady's father. Tanne turned it down.

By now, Blix had made a name for himself as a white hunter. Although six feet tall and powerfully built, he was not Hollywood's image of a tanned, grim-faced hunter eyeing the distant horizon with steely eyes. Bunched cheeks gave him a certain lopsided effect. A close cropped haircut confined a head of otherwise unruly hair. His attraction lay in the delightful smile that lit up his whole face, leaving his companion feeling warmed and responsive. Naturally good manners were only part of his charm. He was always in a good mood. He made people laugh—young, old, natives—everyone.

Rose Cartwright, who knew him well, says he wasn't a womanizer; it was the women who chased him. He easily wore the clothes of his profession: a loose-fitting khaki bush jacket, slouch hat, and moccasin shoes worn without socks. He traveled light, without pose or artifice. Unadorned, he wore neither a watch or an elephant hair bracelet, nor did he carry a knife or binoculars. His natural sight was exceptional. He did, usually, carry a small pair of pruning scissors to snip soundlessly coarse grass and twigs when stalking.

Once, on a trip alone, he heard rumors of an elephant with tusks so immense they left deep ruts in the ground. The natives had nicknamed him "Jaho," the invincible. Blix was intrigued and was determined to see the phenomenon for himself. He followed the tracks daily for a month, but never once caught sight of the legendary bull.

One night, just before dawn, Blix woke up, with difficulty, to muffled shouts. The words "Jaho" and "bananas" somehow penetrated his heavy head. Groping under the pillow for his rifle, he was alarmed to find it gone. Determined nonetheless to see what all the excitement was about, he hurriedly wrapped a blanket around his middle and rushed out across the compound in the direction of the banana fields. Just as morning broke, he discerned the outline of a large gray mass feeding quietly on the edge of a swamp nearby. In the first rays of morning light, he saw the most magnificent pair of tusks he had ever seen, or was ever likely to see. Unarmed, he could only stare in awe. Jaho, on the other hand, quite confident of his invincibility, sauntered off without so much as a backward glance. Blix returned to the village, elated.

His elation was quickly met by reality. In the meantime, the villagers had apprehended the thief, who was Blix's cook. Blix wondered how the man had managed to steal his gun without waking him. Pointing to a small brown stain on the mosquito netting around Blix's bed, the village headman explained that one puff of opium was all that was needed to induce, in the victim of the thief's designs, deep sleep.

A Dutch friend, Mello Versluys, on hearing the story, hired Blix on the spot. Perhaps Jaho had become too confident. Setting out from the very place where Blix had last seen him, they came on him within a week. Versluys collected him. The tusks weighed, in aggregate, 290 pounds.

No sooner had the excitement died down when Blix received a telegram informing him of his mother's illness. Blix was extremely close to his family, writing to them almost on a daily basis. (Sadly, these letters have been burned or lost with time.) On receiving the news about his mother, Blix left immediately, walking 260 miles to Stanley Falls, where he caught the steamer that took him down the Congo River to the Atlantic port of Matadi. His mother died that year, in June 1925 at Dallund in Denmark. Blix stayed on with the family for some months before returning to Africa.

Nineteen twenty-six saw him once again in the Congo's Ituri Forest. His companion on this occasion was Dick Cooper.

The Wambuti are by nature shy. The arrival of a large safari party must have appeared threatening, for every dwelling and village they encountered had been abandoned by its little people. The party could do nothing but patiently await the services of a local guide, without whose knowledge and skill they would have been seriously bereft. With diplomatic maneuvering, a willing guide was at last found. Cooper was frankly amazed by the man's sheer ugliness and diminutive size, but he was equally impressed by his skill in bush craft. He could unravel events by the turn of a leaf or blade of grass. The passage of a leopard, okapi, or forest hog left its mark, barely perceptible to the uninitiated. Every root and plant was distinguished by its edible or healing properties. Blix's own trackers, themselves well versed in bush craft, were also full of admiration and learned a great deal over the years from the Wambuti.

Moving on gradually through the forest to the Katanga

district, they arrived at the small village of Wando, named for its chief. Wando was a great elephant hunter, but a man of cruel disposition. He came out to greet the visitors, followed by a man with both hands missing. Cooper looked horrified. He couldn't take his eyes off those stumps. Wando laughed. He explained that it had fallen on him to sever the hands of his own brother as punishment for having ill-timedly cast an eye over one of their father's harem. He even reenacted the part with a downward swing of his hand. The wounds had been staunched with a hot iron and had certainly healed well. In all events, the two brothers appeared to be the best of friends.

There was a small Belgian encampment not far from the village that Blix and Cooper visited. The Belgians, under a young cavalry officer, Offerman, had begun an elephant-training scheme. It had always been believed that African elephants, unlike their Indian counterparts, were untamable. The results of his efforts would seem to refute this theory. The handlers were rigidly disciplined, and the elephant was treated like a prize thoroughbred. With one handler per elephant, it took twelve months to train the animal to push or pull heavy equipment, including artillery.

No sooner was Blix back in Nairobi than his agent asked him if he would consider taking out a young English couple who were staying at the Club.

On the evening before they were due to leave, a friend of Blix, overhearing their intention to safari with the Baron, drew the man aside to warn him that possibly the most dangerous animal he might encounter would be the hunter, strongly recommending that he travel with extra female company to safeguard his interests and those of his young wife. The poor man, understandably bewildered, readily agreed to take advice. Fearing that this was perhaps normal behavior in the tropics, he allowed Blix's friend to approach a young divorcée, also dining at the Club that evening. The invitation was accepted, and the safari was a great success.

If I were asked to state why we crossed the Sahara by car I should find it difficult to answer, beyond admitting that in doing so we attempted and accomplished something which everybody claimed was impossible.

—Charles Markham

Six

Vagrants North

N 1927, CHARLES MARKHAM, who was by now divorced from Glady (who later married Lord Delamere and became Mayor of Nairobi), was soon to realize his dream of crossing Africa from east to west. He invited Blix to join him on an expedition across northern Belgian Congo by way of the Congo and Ubangi rivers onto Chad by the Shari River. Their objective was to collect species of fish and flora along the rivers for the British Natural History Museum—their excuse to share new experiences and hunting grounds.

They embarked at Stanleyville, present-day Kisangani, in a small, steel boat bought from a Belgian trader, which they renamed *The Vagrant*. Stanleyville has a history of violence since the explorer Henry Morton Stanley first rounded the great bend, bringing with him Zanzibari Arab slavers who made Stanleyville their slaving headquarters. To rid it of the Arabs, the Belgians then turned it into a military garrison. After that, it became the main trading port to ship out rubber and ivory harvested from the surrounding forests. Imposing villas, cafés, and restaurants lined the waterfront, their sweeping gardens overshadowed by the dark, brooding jungle on every side. Dugout canoes plied the river between the right and left bank settlements.

The Vagrant had a carrying capacity of three tons, but it lacked the comfort of a stateroom suite. Blix, the hunter, was no fisherman. Once his initial interest in identifying and logging the catch had abated, the days stretched monotonously ahead. At its outset, the river is nearly a mile wide and in places over nine miles wide. It is dotted with hundreds of sizeable islands, which at times appear to form the opposite bank. The boat followed the natural channels formed under the force of the river's current, which was six to eight knots.

The threat of rain was always with them. The mornings were shrouded in fog, which didn't really burn off until the afternoon, when an eerie light suffused the gloom. Stark flashes of lightning preceded torrential downpours, which abated as quickly as they had started, leaving a musty and cloying atmosphere. Confined to *The Vagrant*'s baking steel hull and droning engine, the passengers found the heavy atmosphere and thick, sweet smell of exotic flowers suffocating. From time to time the leaden form of a crocodile sliding surreptitiously into the water, the darting flight of a winged silhouette, or the snort and grunt of a disturbed hippopotamus were reminders that life on either side of them was tantalizingly out of reach. Their nights were filled with the haunting sounds of the Lokele drum rhythms, which Blix and Charles Markham did their best to drown out with gin.

Three weeks later, the boat reached the border town of Bangui, between the Belgian Congo and French Equatorial Africa. Three hundred miles now separated them from the Shari River in the north, and they now had the awesome task of transporting *The Vagrant* across a land of nonexistent roads to Fort Archambault.

Progress along the first fifty miles was continually reduced to a standstill while trees and bush were hacked down and boulders and stumps removed. They were further impeded by the necessity to backtrack on finding themselves up against an impenetrable cliff or escarpment. Taking stock each evening of the day's insignificant advance, they would wonder, drink in hand, if the whole trip was not a ghastly mistake—something, however, no Englishman would admit. As they moved northward, the terrain opened up to scrub bush and grassland, which in turn became scarcer and more arid. Finally, physically and mentally exhausted, they were ceremoniously launched on the Shari.

Some few miles upstream, disaster struck. The boat collided with a submerged log, shifting the bulk of the cargo to one side. She listed badly, and water poured in. She sank within minutes, taking with her the provisions, cameras, films, and guns. It took ten days to refloat her and salvage what valuable possessions they could. Reduced to poling themselves upriver, the engine's dry batteries waterlogged and useless, they lived off wild duck and geese and slowly made their way toward Fort Lamy, today's Chadian capital of N'Djamena.

Looking around them they found it difficult to believe that this poor country had once been, in the tenth century, the center of the powerful Kanem-Bornu Empire and its fanatically Muslim people, the Kanuri. This tribe drew its strength from control over the trading routes to Egypt in the North, and to the forest kingdoms in the South in what is now southern Nigeria. Gold from West Africa was traded for slaves, ivory, precious stones, spices, and, most important, salt. This was mined north of Timbuctu. While the Kanuri exacted tribute and taxes from caravans passing through its southern domain—Timbuctu, Gao, Kano and Lake Chad—the Tuaregs, a proud, ruthless desert race, turned the trade to their utmost advantage. They led and protected or, conversely, raided the caravans, killing or taking men and women as slaves and the spoils for themselves. The Tuaregs are known as the "blue people" for the Indigo veils the tribal leaders wore as a sign of distinction. In spite of all the hazards, trans-Saharan trading was immensely profitable. A promissory note from around A.D. 950 denotes a debt of 42,000 dinars, approximately $4 million in today's reckoning.

From Fort Lamy there was still some way to go before they reached the main lake basin, an immense stretch of water larger than Belgium. Crossing the lake can be quite deceptive, with winds whipping up its calm waters in seconds. *The Vagrant* tossed about like a cork, coming near to being submerged. Further north there is an archipelago of islands inhabited, while the grass holds good, by nomadic cattle-herding tribesmen who swim from one island to another with their herds, mothers precariously balancing babies on their heads. The women wore nothing but a beaded "cache-sexe" held up by a narrow thong slung about the hip. Many had the hideous beauty scars with raised welts forming intricate patterns on their backs, stomachs, and faces. Blix and Markham spent two months around the lake, fishing and hunting. There was a wealth of bird life: spoonbills, widgeon, teal, plovers, pelicans, cranes, snipe (African variety), and flocks of geese and wild ducks.

Returning to Fort Lamy, they learned that an American working for the International Harvester Company had just passed through on his way to Kano, in Nigeria, having come 3,000 miles from Kenya. Mr. King had let it be known that he intended to sell his vehicle, a modified, boxbody International delivery van, at Kano before going on to Lagos by train. With King's trip the talk at every party in the Fort, somebody keenly suggested that Blix and Markham jettison their boat, buy the truck, and continue on by road. At first the suggestion met with a blank stare, but on talking it over, the idea made sense. Having come so far north, why not continue onto Algiers and Europe rather than head back the

It took Blix and Sir Charles Markham 15 days to cover a distance of 2800 miles from Kano, Nigeria, to Algiers. The "International," the first regular car to complete the journey straight across the Sahara, became a much sought after car and for a long time thereafter almost all vehicles used for hunting in East Africa were of this make.

way they had come? A telegram was composed and more drinks poured.

King soon cabled back, agreeing to sell, in "First Class condition," delivery at Kano. The French, having been so eager to see them off by car, now madly back-pedaled and declared that the whole idea was impossible. For a start, the tires were totally unsuited to soft sand; the car lacked the necessary low-drive gear; it was the wrong time of the year so most of the waterholes would be dry, and high winds and sandstorms would be the norm. If all that and their lack of desert knowledge didn't finish them, bandits would. However, once embarked, Blix and Markham were not to be swayed. Monsieur de Coppet, the governor, acceded and throwing up his hands good naturedly said, "This, *mes amis,* calls for a celebration!"

On the eve of their departure, the governor gave them a splendid farewell party. An assortment of uniformed dignitaries arrived, including several local chiefs, their wives enrobed in all the splendor and color of their stations. The governor, sporting an array of obscure medals on his barrel chest, was seated at the head of the table, while his equally well-endowed wife took her place opposite. To Markham's delight, he was placed on her right. Sir Charles's impeccable French so enthralled Madame de Coppet that she became more and more *decolletée* as the evening progressed. The governor's mistress, a beautiful young *metisse,* viewed the men around her with a certain disdain. Perhaps she knew more about their foibles than they would care to admit? Among the officials seated were the Commandant en Chef des Port, Jetees, Voies Navigable et Chantiers—a rather grand title for someone in charge of a small jetty by the lake where the occasional papyrus canoe was moored—and the Prefet de Police, in a uniform of heavy broadcloth, impressive but impractical in that humid heat. His wife, a vivacious and flirtatious little creature, overestimated her capacity for champagne and left early. Apart from Blix and Charles Markham, the only other nonofficial was the Greek hotelier. L'Hotel Royal could hardly boast a thriving trade, but in the annex he reputedly ran a profitable brothel. Blix found himself seated next to one of the chief's wives, who turned to him and said, "How many cows have you? How many men did you kill?" Blix was about to reply when he realized from her blank expression that she understood no English at all. It was obvious that these few essential questions had been painfully rehearsed. Now that they had been said, she could safely resume her dinner.

Soon, negotiations started in earnest. *The Vagrant* was to be left behind. One of the chiefs hoped to buy it, but when he discovered that the captain, Sir Charles, was not included in the price, he desisted. That left the decision to the governor and the harbor master; the latter won the round. More drinks were poured to celebrate. Everyone got up to leave, save one man who had fallen asleep in the dessert. Blix joined the disdainful mistress, spending the night in her delightful company.

Three days later, on March 24, 1928, they arrived at Kano in northern Nigeria. The city, founded in the eleventh century, had prospered on the strength of its position on the trans-Saharan trading route and was the center for the Hausa tribe. This fine-featured Muslim negro tribe was renowned for its skill in metal work. The mud and wood wall surrounding the city stood as a reminder of this once-thriving desert nation.

The car was found to be in excellent condition, in spite of its arduous 3,000-mile journey, but it lacked tools, spare rims, and tires. The latter items were available, but at a price. Without the tools, Blix put his trust, as the American obviously did, in the infallibility of American workmanship.

The next two days were spent in acquiring, weighing, and listing the following:

2 rolls bedding	100 lbs.
2 small suitcases	50 lbs.
1 food and cooking box	40 lbs.
1 box sundries, camera, etc.	50 lbs.
1 box tools, etc.	30 lbs.
120 (Imperial) gallons petrol	1,120 lbs.
6 (Imperial) gallons oil	60 lbs.
1 native boy	120 lbs.
Blix	160 lbs.
Markham	190 lbs.

At the behest of the English consul in Kano, another evening's entertainment prevented them leaving until well after midnight and forced them to stop a few hours later to sleep off the excesses. Dawn saw them moving again, making good progress along the 300-mile sand track to Zinder in French West Africa (now Niger). A tire puncture caused a two-hour delay and was repaired amid much cursing over the lack of tools. On arrival, the Chef de Cercle, equivalent to the British Resident Commissioner, met them and offered them the use of a house. Zinder, once the base of military conquests, was now a commercial center, and the military was relegated to policing it. The colonel in command of the garrison, a hard-bitten legionary, suggested their best course would be to follow the Niger River as far as Gao, close to Timbuctu. (Timbuctu, in its heyday under Islamic Songhai rule, gave rise to Africa's most ancient university. This, together with its commercial importance, made Timbuctu one of the foremost urban centers in traditional Africa.) From there they would head north. Blix hoped to buy petrol from the French company at Gao.

Leaving Zinder, fifty-six gallons lighter, they initially made good progress on the hardened sand tracks. As the day lengthened, the desert's searing heat registered 125° in the shade, forcing them to stop to cool the radiator, which continually boiled. That night, exhausted, they slept beside the track, then pushed off at dawn, driving as far as possible in the cool of the morning.

Although the roads were marked "passable for cars," the vehicle negotiated steep rises with difficulty, sinking into the soft sand. The heat and the renewed frustration of repairing two more punctures left the three men exhausted, and, too tired to eat, they stretched out beside the car.

On March 30, they arrived at the picturesque town of Niamey, on the banks of the Niger. The Governor provided every facility for them, including the workshops, where they were able to repair tubes and service the car. Surprisingly, the engine required very little oil and, in fact, only consumed a gallon during the entire trip.

Forewarned of bad conditions ahead, they left Niamey with the intention of driving on through the night. But soft sand slowed them down to ten miles an hour, and in places it had obliterated the 100-yard cairn markers. They lost their way in the hills, and Markham felt it prudent to call a halt.

Uncomfortably close to two roaring desert lions, they slept fitfully, gratefully starting out as soon as it was light enough to pick up the tracks that had so eluded them the previous evening. Plowing through deep sand all morning, they eventually reached Gao at midday and made straight for the French company in search of fuel. To their dismay, they discovered there was none, and, worse, that they would have to wait possibly a month for supplies to reach them from Bamako. On a visit to the French garrison later in the day, Blix charmed the commanding officer into letting them plunder government stocks, which they promised to replenish somehow. Meanwhile, the Chef de Cercle had found a guide to show them the way to In Tassit, a waterhole about eighty miles from Gao. The captain told them to follow old tracks all the way, and then they could count on two more waterholes at Tabankort and Asselagh.

With the addition of the new guide, Ali, the services of

the native boy were now superfluous. His scant knowledge of the region and his inability, contrary to assurances in Kano, to communicate in Arabic left him cowering miserably in the back of the car, speechless with fear of this unknown and hostile territory. It was decided, however, to keep him on and send him home from Marseilles, via Lagos, to Kano.

Traveling across country, avoiding thornbush and drifting sand banks, they reached In Tassit in good time and spent the night. With both car and passengers rested and watered, Tabankort came into sight a few hours after dawn. This miserable collection of buildings surrounded by a high mud wall had, until recently, been a military post. It was difficult to imagine anyone living in such a desolate, windswept region without going mad. The heat was awesome and the water salty. They filled up two four-gallon cans and decided to leave the ten-gallon drum until they got to Asselagh. With the drums strapped onto the running board, the car took on the appearance of a merry-go-round, with spare tires and cans arranged symmetrically on either side.

The familiar stone markers had now given way to old tracks made by the trans-Saharan company, whose six-wheeler trucks ferried passengers across the desert. Equipped with wireless sets, they were able to call up their base at Reggan should the need arise.

Sand and flint rock had taken the place of scrub, and the whole landscape shimmered and swelled before them—at times resembling the appearance of a lake bed, only to dry up seconds later. By midday they had still not found water. The intense heat necessitated refilling the radiator every ten miles, and only five gallons of water instead of the required twenty-three were left. Perhaps the captain had misjudged the distance—or had they mistakenly bypassed the well? Neither man dared voice his fear, knowing that to go into the unknown would be unthinkable and that turning back to Tabankort meant going all the way to Gao for fuel. Either way was certain death. Ali, a man of the desert, knew only too well how quickly the desert reclaimed the misfit. He lay crouched in the back of the car moaning, until only the threat of abandonment brought him to heel.

Blix and Markham each wrote his decision on paper so that neither could blame the other for a wrong or hasty move. The two came to a matched conclusion: continue. Jettisoning the bulk of the kit, including provisions and the two empty water cans, they once more broached that vast sea of sand—passing dry camel bones, tokens of abandonment, perhaps omens.

No one spoke as they breakfasted on dry biscuits and a small glass of water, sipping and savoring each delicious drop that had tasted so foul at Tabankort. The sun rose red and angry, foretelling a grueling hot day. The going got worse; the sand in places was so soft that the car had to be jacked up and corrugated iron sheets laid under each wheel. Four paces forward; dig; jack up; underlay; four paces forward. Clawing inches over a 100-yard stretch seemed like an eternity, until they hit harder ground and could once more make faster headway. By evening, they had lost the tracks altogether. Covering ground with ever-increasing circles proved futile. With only a general small-scale map of Africa, the compass was their sole hope. Only half a gallon of water remained. Energy and spirits were at their lowest ebb, and Ali, as though already dead, could not be moved. Tomorrow was another day, and then surely they would be rewarded.

At first light, they set a bearing of due north. The sand, if possible, ran deeper, making their position seem hopeless. By midday they hit old tracks, but relief was tempered by uncertainty. Their mouths were dry and their tongues swollen. Eyes itched and the minutes trickled by. With numbed brains, it took a while to realize that a speck in the far distance had broken the endless miasma of shimmering sand. "Did you see it?" "What is it?" Questions turned to hope. A

AFRICAN ADVENTURES OF AN AMERICAN TRUCK

drum. Water? Accelerate. Do we dare to hope? Touch, push, shake. Empty! Oh! The teasing hand of fate!

To go forward was all that was left to them. Reluctantly filling the radiator for the last time, they continued on in silence, dispirited and depressed. The heat intensified. Steam poured out from under the hood as the car shuddered to gain a grip in the soft sand. Stopping the car to cool the engine, Blix climbed onto a high sand dune in the vain hope of experiencing a changing scene. Incredible! Barely a mile distant lay a drum! Racing and sliding back down the hill, shouting to Markham to get the engine started, he jumped in, spurring Markham and the car onto new strengths. Halfway there, they again sank into soft sand. Impatiently, Blix took to his feet. From the car Markham viewed his progress as in a dream, seemingly immobile one moment and the next shaking drums. "Oh God! Is it petrol or water?"

When Blix reappeared, they all, including Ali, now awakened from death's hypnosis, feverishly dug and laid sheets, finding themselves at last beside the drums. They hastily opened the drum. Water! They drank and drank like demented dervishes, hugging each other with the sheer joy of having come through.

It was the first time that a regular four-wheel vehicle had traversed the Sahara. The car was an "International," mass produced for commercial transport purposes. No improvements or reinforcements had been made to the body or the motor before departure. The previous owner had only modified the cab by changing it to a so-called safari body.

International Harvester became extremely excited by the quality and the performance of their vehicle and produced a sales brochure with the title shown. It described the travels of Mr. King from Nairobi to Kano as well as the Blix/Markham journey from Kano to Paris. The introduction is adventurous: "This is a plain workaday tale of how a plain, workaday American motor truck braved the terrors and bested the trials of a 6600-mile journey across Equatorial Africa and the dreaded Sahara Desert."

Buoyed up by fortune's change, the knowledge that they were still only halfway there did not seem to matter. Eating for the first time with appetite, they now welcomed the next lap across the waterless Tanezruft desert. Every available receptacle was filled to capacity. Before leaving, Blix left five bottles of beer beside the drum for future thirsty travelers.* From then on the going across hard-baked sand and flint rock was smoother—until they reached a dead end, four hours later, after midnight, in front of a fifty-foot sand drift. No one needed any prompting to stop and bivouac there for the night.

As soon as the sun rose, the travelers headed north, skirting around the dune. They drove at full speed throughout the day and night, stopping twice to mend punctures before reaching civilization—or at least the outskirts of Reggan, the trans-Saharan company headquarters. Here they were welcomed by the Hardoines, to whom they owed the forethought of the water drum that saved their lives. They were fed and cossetted, reprovisioned and watered, and the Hardoines waved them good-bye after a good lunch the following day. Heaped stones again posted the way, and with the exceptions of a few soft patches, they reached Adrah, Algeria's most southern military post, that evening.

Here the commanding officer lacked the necessary authority to supply fuel, but he invited them to stay and gave them an excellent dinner. He telegraphed his superior in Algiers, requesting permission to release the required fuel. By the time the answer came back a few days later, the lieutenant had unearthed a four-gallon can of condemned aviation fuel, enough to get them the 170 miles to Timimoun. Under the strain of having driven twenty-hour stretches a day in

*Looking at a recent map of the Sahara, I was amazed to come upon a spot marked "Bidon Cinq" at the very spot where Blix and Markham first hit water. In French "Bidon" is either slang for bottle or means a jerry can; "Cinq" means five.

such harsh conditions, a few days' enforced rest at Adrah was essential.

Anxious not to lose any more time, and with desert temperatures rising daily, Blix and Markham left Adrah after breakfast, reaching Timimoun at half past one in the afternoon. To their surprise this little garrison post, occupied by a handful of Europeans, boasted a charming, white-washed hotel with hot and cold running water. The food was French at its best, and the wine list included vintage crush that had not been seen or tasted in years. The hotel was part of the trans-Saharan company chain throughout North Africa, where tourists were taken on a desert tour in six-wheel vehicles to enjoy the experience of having "crossed the Sahara." The hotel manager was most put out when Blix remarked that they had already not only crossed the desert but were well through it!

Leaving the comfort of Timimoun's hospitality, they drove the rest of that day and night as far as Fort McMahon, 118 miles away. Staying but half an hour, since the fort had been abandoned years before and there was nothing of note to see, they motored on to El Golea. Later, once more in comfort at a trans-Saharan "hotel touriste," they used the time to repair tire tubes.

From El Golea to the next stop at Gardaia, the going got rough, necessitating endless tire changes. However, from Gardaia they hit the well-traveled Route Nationale and got to Laghouat, a large military depot with hotels, cafés, and music halls, in record time. They entered the Hotel Grand dishevelled and dirty, causing a mild sensation. Conversation came to a stop, and all eyes turned disapprovingly to the two wild apparitions. They were fed and refuelled with all speed; manager and clientele were relieved to see the back of them. Subsequently, their early-afternoon roadside siesta was ceaselessly disturbed by anxious passers-by inquiring whether they had broken down.

On the last day, struck by the similarity of the Atlas Mountains to the Swiss Alps, they at last felt as if they were well out of the tropics. They dropped down to Algiers at three in the afternoon. They sank gratefully into the luxurious care of the Hotel Algeria and changed into freshly laundered clothes sent out from Europe to coincide with their arrival.

After 2,818 grueling miles, they must have felt the boat trip to Marseilles was painless. Disembarking with the faithful International, the two men set out immediately for Paris, stopping only for fuel and meals.

On their arrival at the Ritz in Paris, Cockie was there to meet them: "A sight I shall never forget!" The dirt-coated International, displaying an array of tires, hurricane lamps, jerry and water cans, and the odd trophy, caused quite a stir. Crowds gathered around them. Blix and Markham had every reason to be proud. They were the first people ever to have crossed the Sahara in a conventional, stock model, four-wheeled automobile.

That evening the trio celebrated, popping champagne corks and partying until the early hours of the morning. Cockie recalls the relief shown by the hotel's management when, three days later, they finally departed.

Sir Charles Markham left for London.

Blix and Cockie went to Sweden, and there they were married.

I have never regretted anything—except leaving Blix. He was the love of my life.

—Cockie Hoogterp

Seven

Cockie: 1928–1932

O ONE EVER KNEW Cockie by her real name, Jacqueline. She had been nicknamed after coq-a-leeky soup, and the name stuck. She was not a conventional beauty. Bobbed black hair framed a soft round face and wide mouth; her face was beautiful, except for a beaky nose. She adored clothes and dressed cleverly to conceal a plump figure. Her great attraction stemmed from an infectious gaiety. She could see the funny side of everything. Never lost for a word, she could turn a phrase or situation into one of outright hilarity. Fiercely independent herself, she unselfishly recognized the same need in Blix.

Blix loved wild parties and was always attracted to one woman or another. He did everything for his women, and all the money he ever earned was spent on women, parties, friends, and anyone who happened to be around—in that order. Although he was constantly unfaithful, nobody disliked him. He was utterly hopeless with money and very seldom paid, or was able to pay, his bills.

For now, Cockie was his devotee, and he hers. After an exhaustive honeymoon touring Europe and Scandinavia, it

was a relief to be home. Jollity met their arrival in Nairobi, where they downed glass for glass at each round of well-wishing to celebrate their marriage and a new start. Dick Cooper, Blix's first hunting client, had acquired the lease on a 5,000-acre block of land at Babati, in Tanganyika, which he asked Blix, as a friend, to develop and run.

Leaving Nairobi in a decrepit lorry, with a couple of servants balanced precariously on top of a canvas-covered heap of tents and supplies, Blix and Cockie set south across the Athi plains, dropping down from Kajiado into the dry country toward Namanga Hill, which they reached just before sunset. With their backs to Namanga, early the next morning, Longido Hill soon rose out of the plain. It was difficult to believe that only ten years previously this little hill, shrouded in the morning shadow, had seen so much bloodshed at the battle of Longido Ridge.

The joy of traveling in these parts is that, however long the journey might be, there is always a hill rearing out of the mid-distance, or the darker green outline of a stream bed snaking through the plain, each a point of contact to look forward to with the comforting knowledge that there, or just beyond, lies a welcome drink and bath. Game was in abundance, and their progress was punctuated by impala and Grant's gazelle darting across the road, horns held high in defiance. Unaware of the approaching vehicle, a group of Maasai loping casually down the road, deep in thought, would suddenly jackknife to the side. Handlers and load would be pitched forward, only to settle back in a thick layer of red dust. Sometimes they would wave the lorry down, hoping for a lift, although they were clearly heading in the opposite direction. Time was of no importance, and a ride

Blix with Cockie Hoogterp.

anywhere always made for a pleasant change from nomadic wanderings.

That night's rest was to be in Arusha. Its approach skirts the western slopes of Mount Meru, which effectively blocked any view of Mount Kilimanjaro to the east. The travelers headed west the following morning, across some of Africa's most concentrated game country, to Mtu Wa Mbu on Lake Manyara's northern shore, motoring on to Karatu and south over high ground that provided a spectacular view of the lake below, before climbing up over the wooded Mbulu escarpment and down again towards Babati.

Babati, a handful of dukas, lies in flat, dry scrub country surrounded on three sides by hills. Their forested slopes concealed all manner of game, including the unpredictable rhinoceros, whose thunderous approach can send you shinning up a tree a score of times before breakfast.

Much the same as he had done on the farm at Ngong, Blix set about recruiting labor to clear, break land, and plant. They lived under canvas for a while before some sort of house could be built. The resulting shack had a corrugated iron roof to collect water during the rains, since there was no natural source at hand. Although the house lacked the finer comforts, the time spent there was idyllic. Friends dropped in continually. Blix, who knew the country well, took pleasure in showing it all to Cockie, who would accompany him in the evening to shoot for the cooking pot.

November of that year saw the arrival in Arusha of Edward, Prince of Wales, who was on a semiofficial tour of East Africa with his brother, Prince Henry. What better excuse to have a party for everyone at government expense! The district commissioner lost no time in organizing one and invited the entire European community, which actually amounted to only a handful. Arusha Hotel barely accommodated the royal visitors, so guests were left to pitch tents on the grounds.

As Blix was mixing evening cocktails and Cockie was wondering which of her dresses she would wear, the tent flap opened onto a neat, small figure, hand held out in greeting.

"I am the Prince of Wales and would like to make your acquaintance."

"Well," said Blix, "you couldn't have chosen a better moment," and handed him a drink.

Close on his heels stooped Denys Finch-Hatton, with Captain Alan Lascelles and Piers Legh, the prince's aide-de-camp, behind him. The introductions over, drinks were poured and the purpose of the visit discussed.

Prince Edward was keen to hunt lion, and Finch-Hatton had suggested he go and see Blix as the best man to take him out after lion. There existed then a tremendous comraderie between hunters, before the hunting and safari industry became the commercial rat race it is today. Finch-Hatton knew Blix was *the* lion expert and didn't hesitate to recommend him, although it meant sharing the kudos with someone else.

In the meantime, Prince Henry was hunting with Alan Black. Black had originally been employed by Delamere in 1903 to shoot game to feed the farm laborers. To differentiate between Delamere's Somali headman, also a skilled hunter, Black was referred to as the "White Hunter," coining the name for the men of that profession in the future.

Having agreed to assist the hunt the next day, the group went on up to the hotel to dine and dance. Prince Edward liked nothing more than a good riotous evening. He set the pace, and everyone danced until dawn. No one stood on ceremony, least of all an attractive Mrs. Brooke, to whom Prince Edward had taken a liking. She good naturedly accepted friends' ribald comments when, nine months later, she produced a baby boy. Perhaps to keep tongues wagging, the boy later assumed the name Brooke-Edwards.

Cockie headed back to Babati at first light, while Blix oversaw preparations for the coming hunt. Arriving with

It was an impressive group of vehicles that escorted the Prince of Wales from Arusha to the hunting grounds Blix had chosen.

Prince Edward at Babati, delayed by punctures on the way, the party found Cockie fast asleep and blissfully unaware of the royal visit. Blix woke her up with the unsettling news that he had brought everyone home for lunch, hungry! "What am I going to give them? I've nothing but eggs!" Her embarrassment was quickly dissipated by Prince Edward, who suggested helping her scramble them up.

After lunch, they motored to Mount Ufiome (just outside today's Tarangire National Park), not far from Babati, where Blix thought he would have the best chance of a good lion. Early the next morning, the party headed in the direction they had heard lion in the night and came upon the fresh tracks of a single male. In the dawn light, its path left a shadowed impression through the wet grass. As the sun burned off the dew and shadows shortened, the tracks became less obvious, slowing the pace, while Blix sought here a patch of bruised grass or turned leaf, there the faint trace of a pad.

Some hours later, the tracks led out to a thick patch of bush where it was thought the lion would lie up during the heat of the day. Blix's usual beater tactic would have been to place beaters in a semicircle beyond the thicket to drive the lion down to the waiting sportsman. On this occasion, due to short notice, Blix himself had to do the beating. Leaving Prince Edward downwind with Finch-Hatton, he skirted around the top end. Accurately gauging the direction his quarry was lying, he flushed him out toward the waiting gun. The prince collected a good maned lion and was later heard to remark, "Blix has an attitude towards lion like that of the Prophet Daniel."

Delighted with his trophy, Prince Edward arranged to return in a couple of days' time after his official tour of the Dodoma area to the south.

This time Blix wished to be better prepared and went to see his old friend Michaeli, chief of the Wa'Mbulus, to recruit beaters and bearers. It is thought that the tribe is an offshoot of the Watusi of Rwanda and Burundi. Very light skinned, both men and women are tall and fine-boned. Traditionally they are governed by strict codes of conduct; stealing is severely punished.

When Blix arrived in the village, Michaeli himself was out hunting rhinoceros. A large group of warriors were resting, hunkered down with their spears dug in between their thighs. The chief's return was signaled by each man leaping to his feet in respect, simultaneously driving his spear in the ground in front of him. To hold on to a spear while greeting a fellow man was considered aggressive and not done.

At the Prince of Wales' request, Cockie joined the hunt, a light touch to long evenings seated around the camp fire.

Both Finch-Hatton, in the middle, and Blix were impressed with the endurance of the Prince (right) and his willingness to suspend royal etiquette. He did not take advantage of his rank on any occasion.

Prince Edward entertained on his accordion when not listening to tales of past and shared sport. Drink and talk flowed freely. The prince showed no outward signs of the worry he must have felt over the illness of his father, King George V, fully expecting to be recalled home at any moment. As no one could sneak off to bed before him, and he was never in a hurry to do so, Cockie eventually took the situation in her own hands and firmly bade good night, leaving the way open for the rest of the party to follow suit.

The expected telegram arrived before the end of the trip, and the Blixens hosted a farewell lunch for the prince in their Babati shack. This prompted him to draw Blix aside to administer a half-amused admonishment: "You really cannot let your wife live in a shack like this!"

A few weeks after the Prince of Wales' departure, Chief Michaeli received the King's medal for Africa, which he sported with pride, swelling out his chest to show off "my King friend" to everyone he met. Much to her surprise, Cockie received a promised ice-making machine, but such a modern appliance would have to wait for the installation of a generator.

Life back at Singu, as Cooper's farm was known, was interladen with lively social gatherings between neighbors and visitors, either at home or in Babati, where Cockie was *patronne* of a little pub, The Fig Tree. The pub was the result of the generosity of an American friend, Laura Corrigan. Famous for her wealth—which was derived from her husband's steel mills—and her lavish entertainment in a bid to ensnare the rich and titled, Laura also looked after her poorer, albeit titled, friends to uphold standards at all costs.

Babati's community was as mixed and colorful an assortment of people as you would find anywhere, and The Fig Tree was its center. It consisted of a bar, dining room, three detached guest rondavels (sometimes accommodating those incapable of getting home), a provision store, and a post office. All were managed by a Scot, Jock Douglas, who when sober (which was not too often) ran the business with natural shrewdness. Two rogueish Estonians, Karl Nurk and Evald Marks, ran Babati and Hanang Estates, owned by the Earl of Lovelace. Blix had first come across them in the Belgian Congo some years before, soon after they had deserted the Foreign Legion. Swimming ashore at Marseilles from the island of If, the pair had secreted themselves aboard an Algiers-bound ship. From Algiers they crossed the Sahara on foot and camel. The animals perished, while somehow Nurk and Marks survived.

Nurk ran away with Ferdinand Czernin's bride Kiki while

"Fig Trees' Bar" was the favorite watering hole for the farmers around Babati.

they were on their honeymoon in Tanganyika; he later married her in London. Kiki had been the mistress of Ferdinand's father, a diplomat and the Austrian Minister for Foreign Affairs during 1916–1918. When old Count Czernin grew tired of her, he had simply married her off to his son, proving once again his diplomatic genius. For some time she and Cockie provided the only female glamor in Babati.

The district commissioner, de Coursey-Ireland, was killed by elephants in 1931, and his position was filled by Gordon-Russel, whose policy of noninterference suited the Babati community.

Marooned among a staunchly Greek enclave in the Kiru valley, west of Lake Manyara, was the farm of Dr. Alfred Popp of Germany, a Rhodes scholar, and his Russian wife. Popp kept her busy producing babies, whose deliveries inspired a yearly visit to Arusha. She referred to this as her annual holiday.

Mello Versluys, the Blixens' closest neighbor, had appropriately named his farm Holland Estate. He and Blix were long-standing friends and had hunted together in the Belgian Congo. It was Versluys who had the fortune to collect the prized tusks of Jaho the invincible, whose tusks together weighed 290 pounds. Mello, who Cockie named "the little ray of sunshine," due to his hang-dog expression and delight in being the bearer of bad news, had loaned the Blixens his silver Rolls Royce in which to tour Europe on their honeymoon.

Another close neighbor, the Dane Torben Herfort, ran Ndasagu Estate for Ake Bursell, who had come out in 1913 to manage the Blixen property at Ngong. Herfort possessed an enormous appetite for food, drink—especially drink—and young M'Bulu dancing girls. His capacity was such that a friend bet he couldn't consume an entire sheep and a case of large beer (forty-eight large bottles) in twelve hours. Not only did he win, but he then polished off a four-course dinner at the loser's expense. In spite of these indulgences, he had a good brain, was an expert bridge player, and ran one of the most successful coffee farms in northern Tanganyika. When he died, a post-mortem revealed that he had been living for some time almost without any liver function.

Blix's natural inclination to move on and experience changing scenes persuaded him to take up professional hunting again. Together with his friends Philip Percival and Jeff Manley, he formed Tanganyika Guides Ltd.

Philip Percival was an outstanding hunter and brilliant naturalist. He was immortalized as Pop in Hemingway's book, *The Green Hills of Africa.* As founding president of the East African Professional Hunters' Association in 1934, he became known as the "Dean of White Hunters." Jeff Manley handled the business end from Nairobi, out of an office conveniently close to the Norfolk Hotel. Stores, camp equipment, and transport, housed in a shed alongside the Babati airstrip, were supervised by Ben Fourie, mechanic and second hunter to Blix and Percival. The clients usually arrived in Nairobi, where they were met by Manley and wined, dined, and measured up for safari outfits before being flown down to Arusha.

Over this period, Blix and Percival became East Africa's two leading hunters. They got on extremely well and made a good partnership.

When Dick Cooper returned in 1929, it was decided to appoint another manager at Singu, since Blix's safari commitments were taking all his time. He then became Cooper's agent for East Africa. At the beginning of February of that year, Cooper and the Blixens set off on safari to the Belgian Congo.

For some time Blix had mulled over the idea of opening up the part of Tanganyika west of Arusha to tourism, and on his return from the Congo he called a meeting of Babati farmers and put forward his suggestion that they invite the governor of Tanganyika to tour the area. Arrangements were made and a date was set. The governor arrived, accompanied by the commissioner for African Affairs, Philip Mitchell, who was later knighted for his services as the governor of Uganda and

Philip Percival, Blix's good friend and companion, became "the doyen of professional hunters." Early on he claimed that if the habitat of wild animals was limited to national parks their populations had to be controlled. Otherwise the vegetation would be destroyed. Unfortunately no one followed his advice and the result was as he predicted.

Dick Cooper, right, settled in the United States after World War II where he married an American girl, though he kept his farm, Singu, for the rest of his life; here with his Swedish friends Blix, Krister Aschan, and Lalle Ekman.

the Fiji Islands, where Dick Cooper became his military secretary. The official party was escorted to a high vantage point not far from Singu House, where the entire Babati community, armed with food and drink to make the occasion a lively one, had gathered to hear the governor and Blix, their spokesman, deliberate.

The sight encompassed a breathtaking view, at which no one could remain unmoved. The suggestions—to improve roads and postal services, build hotels and rest camps, and implement a stricter control on game poaching—met with loud cheers.

To reach Ngorongoro and the Serengeti plains meant hacking a way through bush and forests of giant nettles and avoiding being charged by numerous ill-tempered rhinoceros. When in time the government did built a road from Oldeani to the rim of the Ngorongoro Crater, as well as a small rest camp, one can only think it was as a direct result of the meeting Blix had engineered on that sunny morning atop his eyrie.

Safaris were now paying handsomely, and the Blixens could afford their own farm. They bought one adjoining Bursell's at Ndasagu. Here they received the visit of a German war pilot, Captain Ernst Udet. Udet was on assignment for a film company and was on a few days leave. Hoping to shoot a buffalo, he had come to Blix for help. After a rather dramatic afternoon being chased by and avoiding charging rhinoceros, Udet shot an excellent trophy. The horns measured forty-eight inches tip to tip.

Cooper was keen to meet the air ace whose war achievements he had heard so much about, so Cockie invited him over to dinner. During a pause in the discussion on the various merits of gun makes, Cooper said:

> Talking of guns, when I was fighting in France in '17, our trenches were repeatedly attacked by German aircraft swooping in low over the defences. Their machine gun fire was devastating—of course we were sitting ducks. For some reason I had my .450 Holland & Holland with me and thought I'd try it out on those buggers!
>
> Nothing to lose. The first one came straight for us, the pilot clearly visible hunched behind his machine gun. I fired some way in front and to my surprise he plummetted down like a pheasant behind me. The second the same. Hardly believing my luck and cheered on by the men, I quickly reloaded and got a shot off at the third just as he passed over. He also went down."

Udet, his eyes transfixed to a spot just above Cooper's head, asked, "Do you remember what the machines looked like? Their markings?"

"I don't remember the markings but they were light, canvas-covered single seaters, and deadly machines."

"Yes," said Udet softly but without reproach, "they were all from my division and I never knew, until now, what happened to them."

No offense had been intended, and none was taken. The room became very quiet as the two officers sat with their thoughts of the waste of those ghastly years, of the mud, stench, and blood. How strange that they should meet in the heart of the Tanganyika bush.

Blix and Cockie would often go to Arusha to party, or sometimes further afield to Nairobi, whose "bright lights" beckoned to Cockie as strongly as the sense of excitement of going to Paris. The new "in" place was Torr's Hotel, nicknamed Tart's Hotel. Torr's had been built by Ewart Grogan, another 1903 settler and pioneer. He had leased it to Joe Torr, who had first arrived in the country as Sir Northrup McMillan's baker. Stung by his future father-in-law's dismissal—"Well, and what have you achieved in life?"—Grogan walked from the Cape to Cairo (the title of his book) to prove he was worthy of marrying his daughter. Although the journey started further north and ended short of Cairo, it was certainly an achievement in 1899.

Behind the porter's desk at the entrance to Torr's four-story, red-brick edifice stood an incongruous wired-in space to accommodate pets. It was not at all unusual to see a lion or cheetah cub snarling in the box while its owner was having a drink. The ground floor encompassed the circular Palm Court lounge where *thés dansants* were held every afternoon to the music of the resident band, caged behind an ornate balcony overlooking the bar below. Grogan himself was often to be seen surrounded by a bevy of beautiful girls listening intently to "the man with the silver tongue."

On his second visit to Kenya, the Prince of Wales was met by Finch-Hatton and Blix at Mombasa and together they traveled by train to Voi.

In the winter of 1930, the Prince of Wales returned to East Africa and was met in Mombasa by the governor, Sir Edward Grigg, and the two hunters Blix and Finch-Hatton. They boarded the Nairobi train, which stopped en route to let off the hunting party near Maktau (the eastern gate of present day Tsavo West National Park). Bidding farewell to Grigg, they headed for camp, which had been set up in advance with every foreseeable comfort.

Fresh spoor does not necessarily mean that the elephant is just round the corner. Elephants walk as they eat, and the pace at which they move belies their seemingly slow and steady gait. Tracking an elephant can mean hours of walking. The tracks do not appear as a deep imprint like those found by Robinson Crusoe in the sand but are more an impression—a slight change in the color of the earth or on a rocky surface, the tell-tale sign of a fallen leaf or a half-broken or chewed twig. Elephant dung is also taken into consideration, as this is deposited at regular intervals along the way, a mass of semidigested woody remains. You know you are right behind him when the droppings are still steaming. But more often than not, the temperature, and therefore the distance still to be endured, can only be gauged by an implanted finger—always the hunter's!

Unlike previous hunts, this time the Prince of Wales was going to have to work for his elephant. The fresh spoor indicated that the elephant, a large one, had passed through at some stage during the night but was obviously heading fast toward the Pare Mountains and might be many hours' walk ahead. The prince showed remarkable stamina; by nightfall they had still not caught up with the elusive pachyderm, and they slept that night beside the track. They kept this up for three more days. The elephant was sighted on the fourth. They could tell at a distance that he was a big tusker by the way he held his head, bowed down with the weight of his ivory. Finch-Hatton got near for a closer look and estimated the tusks at well over 150 pounds each. As so often happens when hunting, just as the hunters moved forward to get into position, a dry twig cracked underfoot and the old bull, lifting his head, swung his body around in one swift movement and was gone. It would have been hopeless to track him again, for once alerted, he would keep going for hours. They had walked seventy miles out in pursuit—seventy slow miles over rugged terrain, tense with every footfall, and seventy miles back. Blix records his admiration of the Prince of Wales, writing:

> There was nothing to prevent the Prince from surrounding himself with all possible luxury and comfort but he is notoriously not that sort of man. Despising all effeminate softness in others, he makes the greatest demands on himself. I can assert without hesitation that he is one of the three or four toughest sportsmen I have been out with. Perhaps the toughest of them all.

At the end of the safari, the Griggs arranged a dinner party at Government House. The other guests included Lord Francis and Lady Scott and their niece Alice, who was visiting the country with her friend Marye Pole Carew. Alice would later marry Prince Henry to become the Duchess of Gloucester.

Francis Scott was the younger son of the Duke of Buccleuch and had been aide-de-camp to the viceroy of India, the earl of Minto, whose daughter Eileen he married. The Scotts came to Kenya after the war and settled at Rongai, 130 miles west of Nairobi, where they built an imposing two-story house at the foot of Londiani Hill, called Deloraine—a rarity in those days of hastily erected, deep veranda bungalows. Breakfasting off an exquisitely appointed table at Deloraine, at 7,000 feet above sea level, with the early-morning mists swirling up behind the house, they found it difficult to believe they were in Africa. Together with all Eileen Scott's English country house accoutrements had arrived her lady's maid, Loder, and a governess for the two Scott daughters. Loder later became housekeeper at Muthaiga Club, where she was held in fearful respect by both the African staff and members, severely disapproving of the latter's nocturnal antics and muttering loudly "'Airpin's in 'is bed again!" Members thought they had caught her out when, in the middle of the night, screams of, "Out! Out! You filthy beast!" brought inquisitive heads poking around every bedroom door, wondering who could be making an indecent assault on the old girl. They were disappointed, for it was only Loder seeing off a beetle that had been unwise enough to find its way into her bed.

Between professional safaris, it would be typical of Blix's generosity for him to take friends, or even friends of friends, out after game just for the joy of sharing the company and the sport. Open house was the norm, with Cockie dispensing drinks and laughter. The small room was so tightly packed that moving to the drinks table was usually a feat in itself. This went a long way to preserving the gin bottle; no bad thing, considering they were broke more often than not. Most people, used to the vagaries of cars breaking down and long distances, brought their own liquor. The monotony of roadside waiting could always be dispelled with a hip flask or two.

On the whole, professional clients tended to be American, or married to American money, for they could afford the time and the expense. Safaris lasted from one month to three. A meticulous organizer, Blix never left anything to chance. Fly camps, fuel depots, airstrips, provisions, and staff were always laid out well in advance. He would also take the time to reconnoitre an area thoroughly beforehand to check on waterholes and general game movements.

Freddie Guest, a close friend of Dick Cooper, had married a wealthy American and arrived with his family by private plane, on loan together with the pilot, Captain Preston, from the Duchess of Bedford. Over the years the Guests became very close friends of the Blixens, although Mrs. Emy Guest reserved her judgement, for she never took kindly to Blix casting a knowing eye over her attractive daughter, Diana.

For the first leg, they camped in the Serengeti on the Mbalangat River. The hunt went according to plan, except for one amusing incident; although at the time the family hardly found it so. Early one morning, watching a magnificent lion drinking from one of the pools in a drying stream bed, Blix suggested they return in the late afternoon, for if they left him undisturbed, he would probably rest up nearby.

He had obviously fed well off a kill during the night and would be thirsty.

That afternoon he placed Raymond, the younger son, in position to shoot on the opposite bank, while the rest of the party hid at a safe distance behind an ant hill to observe and record the scene on film for posterity. Blix and his bearers noisily beat through from the top end towards Raymond. A low growl, followed by the alarmed call of yellow-neck taking to the air, announced the lion's presence. Then silence. Blix reached the edge of the riverbank, still eerily quiet. No sign of the Guests. "Oh God," he thought, "where the hell have they all gone?"

Suddenly, a strangled whimper betrayed their presence high in a clump of trees beside the ant hill.

"What happened to you?" laughed Blix.

"You said there was only one. Hell, there were nearly forty of them! All different sizes and coming straight for us."

"You must have got some good action then."

"Action! For a moment it was touch and go *who* got the action," gasped Guest. "Get us down. I need a strong drink!"

The party then headed back to camp, feeling in some way guilty at having turned tail on the first sign of danger.

Before starting the second leg, the Guests flew with Blix and Cockie to Nairobi, where they based themselves at Muthaiga, meeting many of the Blixens' friends. It was just before Christmas and the Club was filled with up-country members down for Race Week. Champagne and the festive spirit flowed. Dances went on until dawn five days a week. The Americans partied with as much gusto as any up-country farmer bent on making up for lost time. Freddie Guest, a giant of a man, could consume a staggering amount of drink before, during, and after dinner. Even Blix, himself a good drinker, was impressed by the sheer quantity the man put away, but he never once saw Freddie drunk.

Leaving the family to their own buccolic devices, Blix

When my grandfather Fredrik Bonde and his cousin Carl visited Kenya my parents took them on a so-called "social tour" to see friends and acquaintances throughout the country. Among others they visited Lord Errol at "The Djinn Palace" by Lake Naivasha, where things usually were very lively.

Next to Lord Errol in white shorts is my grandfather and his cousin. My father is seated to the far left next to an unidentified man with a camera and next to him is my mother. The lady in the black blouse is Alice de Trafford, a well known personality in the high-spirited group called "The Happy Valley Set." The woman to the right is also unidentified.

headed back to Tanganyika to prepare for the second leg. Again he turned to the Wa'Mbulu Chief Michaeli for help, advice, and the loan of skilled trackers.

Reading Blix's safari recollections, one is amazed how well he recalls every detail of any hunt and the country over which they hunted. On this occasion, he was intent on finding out from Michaeli about any big rhino in the vicinity. Apparently there were two, one that had left a track indicating a broken toe and the other a stiff leg. Shortly after the Guests rejoined the hunt, Winston collected the rhino with the broken toe and his brother, Raymond, the other. Winston's had a record horn, measuring thirty-two inches.

Cockie was especially relieved to see the end of the Guest safari, effectively closing a chapter on Blix's infatuation for the young Diana. Life quickly resumed its routine course. But not for long. A steady stream of friends and visitors arrived to stay. The Scotts came, Francis taking time off from his political commitments. He was to be elected a year later to the Legislative Council, leading the settlers' cause where Hugh Delamere had left off.

Another visitor, but an unlikely Tanganyika-bound traveler, came in the demon form of Raymond de Trafford, a member of the Happy Valley social set. Luckily, his visit did not coincide with the Scotts', who took a dim view of the group and its scandalous, dissolute behavior. Witty, attractive, well bred, and well read, Happy Valleyites were relentless in their pursuit to be amused, more often attaining this through drink, drugs, and sex. When the writer Evelyn Waugh visited Kenya in 1931, he and Raymond struck up a cosy friendship and corresponded afterwards. "Something of a handful," admits Waugh, "very nice but so BAD and he fights and fucks and gambles and gets disgustingly drunk all the time." Raymond's brother Humphrey, despairing of his younger brother's wayward appetites, proposed a "final solution": "If you agree to be castrated I'll give you ten thousand pounds."

Raymond considered a moment and replied, "For five thousand pounds I'll have one ball removed."

That offer was turned down.

The one trait Blix simply hated was snobbery. During a visit to Sweden in 1930, the Blixens were invited to a grand wedding hosted by one of his ex-girlfriends, who had become insufferably snobbish as the years had gone by. Well pleased with herself for having cornered a *Fürst* (German prince) to marry off to her daughter, she had invited as many titled guests as she could muster. When Blix caught up with his hostess at the reception, he complimented her on the perfect arrangement and magnificent aristocratic turnout, adding, "I'm so glad Fürst Fuller could make it, too."

"Another prince! Do I know him?" she asked, looking hurriedly about her. "Where shall I put him? This ruins my seating plans." Recovering her poise, she said, "Fürst Fuller you say? I'm not sure I remember exactly what he looks like. Do point him out to me, Bror."

"But surely you must know Fürst Fuller!"

Eagerly scanning the expanse of lawn before her, the distraught woman was by now close to tears. Blix laughed. Pointing a finger at himself, he slowly repeated "Fürst Fuller," a play on words in Swedish, "the first to get drunk."

Whether Blix was "Fürst Fuller" on the occasion of the funeral of Lalle Ekman's mistress is moot. Lalle and Thyra Ekman farmed just outside Arusha. Lalle would occasionally take clients out on safari. One of these, a handsome Russian lady, obviously got more out of her White Hunter than she had bargained for. On their return, he built her a small house on the farm. This arrangement did not withstand the test of time. The lady committed suicide soon afterward. Lalle asked Blix to come to the funeral, suggesting they meet at a hotel in Moshi to bolster themselves with a few pink gins before making their way to the graveside. Lalle's wife and four daughters, who had by this time decked themselves out in the Russian mistress' black lace, stood beside the grave. The

Gustaf Kleen (nicknamed Romolus, having been born in Rome) was the son of Blix's sister and became one of Blix's very best friends. Romolus stayed in East Africa until the middle sixties. He was a well known and competent cattle rancher and an excellent rider who won many victories on the race track. Here on the front steps of Singu House with Blix in 1931.

coffin was lowered, and Blix stepped forward to read the last evangelical rites—whereupon he lost his footing and tipped headlong over the edge.

In May 1931, Denys Finch-Hatton was killed in an aeroplane crash at Voi. Tanne left the country shortly afterward, a broken woman. Finch-Hatton's death, combined with the loss of her farm, made for great bitterness, much of it directed in retrospect at Blix. It was as if the fault lay squarely at his door for having instigated a life in Africa which, in the end, brought her much pain and little happiness.

Just before she left, Blix's nephew, Gustaf Kleen, came out from Sweden. What better introduction than to see the country through Blix, whom he joined on an all-female safari. Romolus (as Gustaf had always been called, having been born in Rome) so loved it all that he decided to stay on.

By this time, Blix had earned a reputation as a hunter without equal, and a womanizer bar none. One client insisted he pen a guarantee not to bed his (the client's) wife. On this particular occasion, both Cockie and Romolus were present, so the situation never presented itself.

Cockie was such good entertainment value. After a long and tiring day's hunting, she could take the heat off Blix, allowing him a few minutes' quiet relaxation on his own. His profession necessitated living at close quarters with comparative strangers. A typical hunting day would start well before cock's crow and not finish until after the brandy had been drained and sleep took over.

In the middle of a safari with two young Americans from Chicago, Simpson and Armour, Blix received a telegram from Simpson's father announcing his imminent arrival in Nairobi en route to the Far East. Apart from dropping in on his son, Simpson, Sr., hoped to bag the Big Five—elephant, rhinoceros, buffalo, lion, and leopard—in under a week and was prepared to pay any amount to do so. Most hunters would have turned him down flat. Blix enjoyed a challenge. He set his best trackers to work, cleared landing strips, arranged well-stocked camps in several areas, and hired aircraft. It all paid off. Simpson was able to travel eastward, his objective fulfilled. The game department later brought in a ruling that the Big Five could only be collected over the course of a month's safari, a ruling intended to stop those as zealous as Blix from achieving the near impossible.

His next challenge was to get Cockie back to Nairobi in time to meet an aeroplane. Even in those casual days, Imperial Airways did not wait for latecomers. In November 1931, just before she flew to England, the rains came with a vengeance and continued to pour out of the sky day after day. Lake Manyara spread out over the Mbugwe plains, and the main Arusha road disappeared under two feet of water. Blix dispatched a runner to Chief Michaeli with a request for a hundred of his strongest men. On their arrival, Blix placed fifty aside along the length of two sturdy ropes hitched to the front bumper. With Cockie safely cocooned among the luggage, Blix plugged the exhaust, jumped in behind the wheel, and gave the word. The men pulled the car, dragging it through fifteen miles of water to the haunting accompaniment of M'bulu warrior songs. Once through, the Wa'Mbulus headed home with no more sign of exertion than if they had played a competitive game of tug-of-war. Further drifts and washouts were negotiated by the simple expedient of forging new tracks. Cockie caught her plane on time. Nobody else was able to make it for several weeks. The landscape was strewn with half-submerged vehicles, bearing witness to those who had tried.

On his way home, Blix called in on an old friend near Arusha who had just come out of hospital following a lion incident. At sixty-five, Colonel "Jim" Gray had long since hung up his big game rifles. Repeated cattle raids and the loss of a prize heifer finally forced him to confront the marauders head-on. Drawing on his Indian experiences, Gray built a "machan" above one of the cattle pens. Sure enough, on the first night, three shadowy feline forms materialized out of the bush and came toward him. Gray fired at all three. When the ring of gunfire had subsided, he neither heard nor saw any sign. Unsure whether he had killed all three, he waited until daybreak before climbing down. The following morning, he found two of the lions stone dead. The third had obviously been badly wounded, judging by the bloodied tracks that led off to the bush. Gray followed them wearily. Barely ten yards in, the wounded lion sprang out. Gray fired, but too late—the lion was already on him, his teeth firmly clenched around the old man's arm. Accepting the inevitable, Gray allowed himself to be dragged off.

Strange are man's thoughts at the hour of death. All Gray

could think of at that moment was Hilaire Belloc's Victorian cautionary tale "Jim," who ran away from his nanny at the zoo and was eaten by a lion:

You know—at least you ought *to know,*
For I have often told you so—
That children never are allowed
To leave their nurses in a crowd;
Now this was Jim's especial foible,
He ran away when he was able,
And on this inauspicious day
He slipped his hand and ran away!
He hadn't gone a yard when—
Bang!
With open jaws a lion sprang,
And hungrily began to eat
The boy, beginning at his feet.
Now just imagine how it feels
When first your toes and then your heels,
And then by gradual degrees,
Your shins and ankles, calves and knees,
Are slowly eaten, bit by bit.
No wonder Jim detested it!

Fortunately, before Gray had come to the end of Belloc's morbid moral saga, he realized that the grip on his arm had loosened. The lion was dead. The last bullet must have done the job. Weak from shock, loss of blood, and excruciating pain, Gray managed to drive his old Ford to the Arusha hospital. At home again, Gray hung up his rifle, with a piece of broken lion tooth still embedded in the stock, over an inscription relating, not to Belloc, but to Sampson's fight with the lion from the Old Testament.

The next prominent guest on Blix's agenda was Alfred Vanderbilt. Vanderbilt was a keen sportsman but was incredibly unlucky. Blix took him out after elephant in his favorite hunting area around Voi. They followed the tracks of a huge bull but in a month's hunt never came close to him. In the meantime they had gone through several pairs of shoes, crashed an aeroplane, and demolished three vehicles. Blix fully expected to be fired any day, but Vanderbilt was determined to continue.

One afternoon while they were out bird shooting, a rhinoceros charged out of nowhere and headed straight for Vanderbilt. Armed with only a shotgun, he could do little but flee. Blix's bearer fortunately had the heavy rifle, which he handed to Blix. The rhinoceros fell two feet behind Vanderbilt, who had been running flat out. Fleeing from a charging animal is always a mistake: you provide it with a clearly visible and inviting target and cannot afford the time to stop and look back. More people are killed by dangerous game this way than any other.

That evening, Vanderbilt, recovered from the afternoon's excursion, turned to Blix and said, "If I come back next year how long would we need to get a big elephant?"

"Two months should do it."

"O.K., let's make it three. This is the first time I've been after something money can't buy and I've enjoyed every minute."

Ironically, Freddie Guest and his daughter Diana returned shortly afterward. In the same area that Vanderbilt had been outwitted, Blix and Percival found them four elephants in just under a week. Each tusk averaged over a hundred pounds. Perhaps the huntress goddess Diana had had a hand?

Blix was the first professional hunter to hunt the Tsavo area, a vast stretch overreaching today's Tsavo National Park from beyond the Tiva River in the north to the area around Voi as far as Kenya's southern border. The Wakamba tribe predominate to the west, closely followed by the Waliangulu or Wasanye to the east. The latter, known as the "Elephant People," were a hunter race living entirely off game, elephant in particular. The Liangulu bow is unique in Africa, measur-

A steady stream of Blix's and Cockie's many friends were drawn to "Singu Estate"—not only because they were always welcome but also because of the great charm of the hosts.

ing nearly six feet and weighing close to a hundred pounds, with a heavier pull than the English longbow. To my knowledge, no European has ever managed to draw it. The arrow heads are tipped with a poison from the sap of the Akocanthera tree, which is boiled up. To determine the strength of the brew, the hunter makes an incision on his upper arm and allows the blood to flow. Placing a drop of the deadly poison at the end of the line of blood, he watches it fizzle up the arm, scraping it off just before the poison reaches the incision. The speed at which the venom travels is a measure of its deadliness.

Simba, Blix's best tracker, was a Liangulu. He had been with Blix for many years, in the course of which he had made enough money to buy three wives and some cattle—a departure from the old ways. Together they had twice crossed the African continent as far as Timbuctu and traveled by sea from Dakar to Mombasa via the Cape. Although Simba had seen

some of Africa's more fertile pastures, home would always be the monotonous dry bush country by the Voi River.

From living off the meat of elephant, the Liangulu hunters naturally progressed to poaching. Later, rather than serve prison sentences, many "volunteered" their services as trackers to ferret out those poachers who had still not joined the side of conservation. (Hekuta, Simba's son, became one of the leaders of antipoaching units for David Sheldrick, the Tsavo Park Warden.) A Mkamba hunter, Makula, was probably the greatest poacher ever. He had seen some huge ivory in his time and taught Blix a great deal. They would talk for hours about the country, seasonal and permanent waterholes, and the ins and outs of the illicit ivory trade.

On one of Cooper's annual visits, Blix took him into a new area after elephant. Hacking their way through sansevieria and "wait-a-bit" thorn the entire morning, Blix called a halt. They poured drinks and settled back in folding chairs in the

shade beside an old game trail. Suddenly an old rhinoceros exploded down the path, puffing and snorting. Everyone jettisoned their drink and scattered while the rhinoceros, head down, charged straight into the lunch box, collecting a camp chair on the way. Fortunately, he kept going—camp chair balanced on his horns.

When Cockie returned from England, it was obvious that Blix's affections had wandered again. "We never had any rows about it. He was a wonderful—unfaithful—husband," Cockie told me recently. "And the best lover I ever had."

The object of his interest was Beryl Markham, who had been married briefly to Charles Markham's brother, Mansfield. Brought up by her father, she was more comfortable in a man's world, where she made her living flying. Although she made twice as much money flying reconnaissance trips for Blix, she also accepted that the dangers were twice as great. Together they flew all over the Voi area, sharing hardship and

Eva Dickson and her friend Littan on their way to see Blix.

excitement alike. They became extremely close, and, knowing them, were probably lovers. For over two months, they explored the country between Dakadima hill and the Galana River—a country of bush, fever, drought, siafu ants, and sansevieria, described by Beryl as "that placid but murderous weed, jutting up like an endless crop of sabres. Land on sansevieria and your plane is skewered like a duck pinned for taxidermy—land in it and walk away."

In August 1932, Cockie left again for England, this time to see her mother, who was seriously ill. Blix could not join her, as he was committed to taking out the Law brothers, who owned a farm nearby, which was managed by Romolus Kleen.

The day before he was due to leave, a car drew up on the lawn. Out stepped two young strangers who introduced themselves in Swedish.

"Baron Blixen?"

"Yes?" said Blix inquiringly.

"I'm Eva Dickson, and this is my friend, Littan. We have just come from Dar-es-Salaam and are very thirsty."

Dar-es-Salaam to Babati is a journey of more than 400 miles over impossibly rutted roads, so Blix could understand the need for a drink. But why the visit?

"I'm delighted to meet two such charming ladies, but what brings you all the way to Babati?"

"Ah," smiled Eva, "to meet *you*!"

Blix was flattered, the spell began, and the die was cast. Eva Dickson was no ordinary woman. Determined not to lose sight of her, he persuaded the Laws to allow the two women to join the safari.

The safari was not conducted with the hunter's usual single-mindedness, and Blix, distracted, was impatient to see it finished. He took the two women to Nairobi, where Littan met Gustaf Mohr, a friend of Tanne's, whom she later married. That left Blix and Eva.

When Blix met Cockie at the airport with Eva, he suggested they should all go up-country for the weekend.

Cockie for once was not amused. It was a new threat. With a pang of jealousy, she said, "What! The three of us? There's a limit. There will be only two of us. Take your choice."

Blix chose Eva, and there ended his marriage to Cockie.

Recently Cockie told me: "I was a fool. Had I stuck it out, it [the affair] would have been over in six months. I have never so regretted anything in my life as leaving Blix."

After their marriage broke up, Blix returned to Babati less and less. The sparkle had gone out of Babati life. And Blix's favorite proverb could well be applied: "Life is life and fun is fun, but it's all so quiet when the goldfish die."

Bror was the toughest, most durable white hunter ever to snicker at the fanfare of safari or to shoot a charging buffalo between the eyes while debating whether his sundown drink will be gin or whisky.

—BERYL MARKHAM

Eight

Eva and Beryl: 1932–1938

EVA DICKSON AND BERYL MARKHAM were alike in spite of diverse backgrounds. They shared a common love of excitement and danger. Independent and unafraid to try the unknown and the untried, they would today be labeled "liberated," a term that conjures up a forced defiance against anything that smacks of machismo. Beryl and Eva's natural bent simply lay in doing things for the sheer fun of it. And they both fascinated Blix.

Eva, the younger of the two by three years, was born in 1905 in Sweden and was brought up at Ljung Castle. She was Gillis Lindstrom's cousin. Her father ran a large stud farm and bred racehorses. The children had a very strict upbringing, but it failed to dampen a mind bent on new challenge and change. At nineteen Eva married Olle Dickson, a keen racing driver and proud owner of a prestigious Ballot, capable of reaching the unheard-of (in 1925) speed of one hundred miles an hour. He introduced Eva to rallying, and she soon shared his passion. Together they raced, and before long she outshone Dickson at his own game. This brought them to a parting of the ways, for Olle quickly rebelled at being called

Mr. Eva Dickson. They parted as friends. Olle fondly remembered her as "a great spender, adventurous, brave, full of life and fun. She just loved to cause a sensation."

After the divorce, Eva bought into a large fashion house in Stockholm, disrupting its ordered existence, modeling the creator's designs back to front, his hats upside down. She certainly did cause a sensation. Sales doubled.

Before long her passion for motor cars sidetracked her again. At that time, women were barred from competing in the Monte Carlo Rally. Eva simply avoided the ruling. She entered under an assumed name, disguising herself behind a large theatrical moustache, though in mid-winter her face and figure were concealed by a wealth of fur.

She had a string of devoted admirers, but none made a lasting impression. She wanted an equal. From her brother, Ake Lindstrom, Eva had heard a great deal about the adventurous womanizer, Baron Blixen, and his life in Africa. Why not give it a try?

I believe she was unprepared for the intensity of his love for her. Although it was reciprocated, she was troubled and afraid, afraid to be possessed and yet angry at allowing herself to succumb so easily. Troubled because she knew deep down that if she left before she were ready, Blix would transfer his affections elsewhere.

The chance to reassert herself came once again with a challenge. At a party at the Club, someone wagered her she couldn't cross the Sahara in an ordinary motor car within thirty days of leaving Nairobi. For a meager case of champagne, she jumped at the opportunity. The thirty days would only include actual driving days. Unforeseen events would not be held against her, and she could take a companion. Eva

chose a Somali, Hassan Ali, and together they left Nairobi in a six-cylinder Chevrolet on November 20, 1932.

Traveling partially along the same route Blix and Sir Charles Markham had covered five years previously, they reached Fort Archambault without mishap. There they stayed with a Swedish missionary—who did not appreciate Eva flinging his best leather-bound Bible at a snake.

Trouble really started south of Fort Lamy. The road had been washed out and would be impassable for another three weeks. Their alternative was to drive via Bongor, in Chad, through the northern Cameroon corridor onto Kano and Nigeria. On reaching the Longone River, they found the bridge down. Hassan was dispatched to a nearby village to consult the headman, who arrived with a gathering of curious, naked onlookers.

Slowly opening and closing his eyes to emphasize the seriousness of their position, the chief threw up a hand and said, "Nothing to be done, Madame. You must wait the commandant at Bongor. Only he and engineer build bridge." Adding, as he looked at this determined white woman, "Perhaps, Madame, if you see the commandant yourself?"

"How far is Bongor and how do we get there?" Eva asked.

Pointing in the general direction, he said, "Five hour by horse."

He then barked out a series of orders that must have included finding a guide, who arrived shortly with a spare horse in tow.

Fording the river astride a horse was no problem, but no sooner had they shaken off the water when the guide's horse reared up, whinnying shrilly. A lion was crouched in the grass beside the path, watching. The guide took off and Eva, terrified, could only scream and flap her arms menacingly. It seemed to produce the required effect, and the lion pushed off. The guide reappeared as though nothing had happened, and they were on their way again.

By midday, Bongor was still out of sight. The little water they had carried had long been drained, and Eva was beginning to feel weak from thirst. In the late afternoon, their spirits were renewed at the sight of a small village shimmering in the distance. It was not Bongor.

Here they gratefully accepted a muddy brown offering that passed for water. Inquiring of the villagers of the distance ahead, they gathered by the pantomime of gestures describing sunrise and sunset that Bongor was still a good twelve hours away. Eva refused to believe them and set out once more.

At nightfall they reached a large barrack-like building but were told that Bongor was still forty kilometers on. Leaving someone to take care of the horses, Eva and her companion, overcome with tiredness, lay down by the fire to sleep.

The commandant at Bongor could not have been more helpful or indeed more surprised by Eva's visit. "For you I will summon an army to build the bridge tonight." The bridge was repaired three days later. Thanking the commandant and villagers, Eva and Hassan departed. They motored to Kano, where a broken rear spring was replaced.

Permission to cross the desert via French forts was granted by the commandant at Maradi. He was reluctant to let them go, for visitors seldom dropped in, and one so beautiful was rare indeed. "You and the desert," he said, "are more beautiful than anything I know. The desert is also most dangerous and I would be unwise to let you go."

"Yes," agreed Eva, thinking the commandant equally dangerous, "but if you do not allow me to cross I will lose my bet and with it an entire case of champagne."

"Champagne! Why then, of course you must go."

Waking up at Niamey one morning, Eva found Hassan waiting by the car, looking slightly sheepish. "What's up, Hassan?"

Swivelling his eyes to a point somewhere behind him,

Eva's faithful companion Hassan probably wondered more than once about the purpose of the Sahara excursion, since it resulted neither in riches nor fame.

Hassan replied, "Oh, Madame, a Tuareg chief wishes to buy you for wife."

"What's he offering?"

"Thirty camels. Very good price. But you must not accept."

At that point her suitor detached himself from the side of the house, white burnoose swelling in the breeze, and stood before her. Coal-black eyes stared out beneath an indigo turban, and for a moment nothing moved. She was glad that at least he was a handsome chieftain, but she emphatically shook her head. To her relief, the Tuareg slowly nodded and

In retrospect it is interesting to note that Eva's desert crossing caused no particular stir outside Sweden. She was, after all, the first woman to cross the Sahara in a regular car.

smiled, offering her a ring delicately worked with silver filigree. It occurred to her that the gift was appropriate, for it was nearly Christmas.

Motoring on, they passed Gao and reached Tabankort, the last fort before entering the real desert. Blix had told her the water there was undrinkable but worth stocking up so as not to be caught without, as he and Markham had been. Of course, Eva was traveling at a much cooler time of the year. The track, too, was better marked, but the character of the sand remained unpredictable.

A day or two out of Tabankort, the unfamiliar drone of an

aeroplane broke the desert silence. Sticking her head out of the window, Eva was amazed to see it come in low over the car and land a short distance away. She then realized it was the French aviator, Vicompte de Sebour, whom she had met in Nairobi.

"Just thought I'd look in on you. Sure you're O.K.? I can always give you a lift to Algiers."

"No! We're fine," Eva assured him. "And we'll win that bet yet!"

As de Sebour disappeared into the northern sky, Eva wondered if Blix had sent him.

Exactly halfway between Tabankort and Reggan lies the spot where Blix and Markham had found the drum of water that saved their lives. The trans-Saharan company had since made Bidon Cinq a fuel and water depot. Eva refueled and filled up with fresh water.

If one suffers from heat by day, the discomfort is equally intense at night. The night at Bidon Cinq was no exception. Eva awoke in the morning with hands cracked and bleeding from frost.

"If you reach Reggan, you've made it," Blix had told her. However, there were still 1,400 miles ahead. At Reggan, Eva met up with the Hardoines, who were delighted to have news of Blix. At dinner that night, Eva listened to the horror stories of those who hadn't made it.

Eva and Hassan did. The faithful Chevrolet arrived in Algiers twenty-seven driving days later, on December 28. The bet was won, and Eva was the first woman to have driven across the Sahara.

A year after Eva was born, Charles Clutterbuck moved to Kenya with his daughter Beryl, aged four. Her mother remained in England. Forests of tall cedar, podo, and bamboo formed a backdrop to the beginnings of a feudal village between the Mau Escarpment and the Rongai Valley. Here

Clutterbuck, a steeplechaser and trainer, built the first racing stables in East Africa, importing stallions and breeding mares from England and Abyssinia, making "a farm out of nothing and everything." Beryl grew with the farm and the inevitable changes European settlement and influence brought. She was the only white child within 200 miles. Her playmates were the children of the Nandi Moran, their games hers, their fathers her tutors. Under the tutelage of Arap Maina, she learned not only to read spoor and follow a blood trail but acquired the gift of observation and the knowledge to use her senses and act instinctively on them. Although her father did his best to give her some sort of formal education, hunting forest hog barefoot or watching, unseen, over a salt lick were infinitely preferable pastimes to studying English or arithmetic. Apart from Kibii, Arap Maina's son, her closest friends were a tough bull terrier cross and her father's horses, which she fed, groomed, and rode, sometimes sleeping in with a foaling mare. At her father's side, she became as conversant with blood line and form as she was with the well-beaten paths around her.

At seventeen, life for nature's child ended. The year 1919 was a war-ravaged year without rain and without crops. Charles Clutterbuck, like so many, was bankrupt. He gave Beryl the choice of leaving Kenya with him to start again in Peru or staying in Africa to continue what he could no longer carry on—a life of training and racing thoroughbreds.

Riding out on Pegasus, her father's last gift, with her possessions packed in two saddlebags, Beryl left the farm and childhood forever. She rode across the bleak Molo downs to a job and adulthood.

Although young and inexperienced, her uncanny sense for horses attracted clients, and soon she was an established trainer. Kibii, now a Moran warrior with the Morani name Arap Ruta, joined her in the new role of servant and protector; he stayed with her throughout her days in Kenya.

Success led her on to Nakuru and finally to Nairobi, where she met and married Mansfield Markham, Charles' younger brother. The marriage lasted barely two years. It had supposedly been her second; the first had lasted only a few months.

With racing success behind her, Beryl's thoughts now turned to flying. Her tutor and mentor was Tom Black, whom she had first come across out riding one morning in Molo. She stopped briefly to chat while he pulled wires from under the bonnet of a broken-down car and learned he had a farm nearby and a dream to own his own aeroplane. They met again some years later in Nairobi, upon his return from London. His dream had come true. The aeroplane was his own. "You will fly this plane," he told Beryl.

"Me? Fly?"

"Of course. I've seen it in the stars."

She started the following morning, his first pupil.

One thousand hours and eighteen months later, she flew passengers, cargo, and mail all over East Africa by compass, instinct, and the very senses she had unconsciously acquired at Arap Maina's side.

The idea of spotting game from the air had been conceived by Denys Finch-Hatton and Blix and was executed by Beryl. After Denys's death, Tom Black attempted to dissuade her from continuing, in spite of the remunerative pay package. Writing to her from London, he said, "You won't listen but financial worry may be eased by one or two safaris—as a steady business it's sheer madness and damnably, bloodily dangerous."

Beryl Markham became a most excellent pilot and the crowning achievement of her career was her solo flight over the Atlantic from east to west.

As she brooded over the contents of Tom's letter, Arap Ruta dropped a folded telegram on her desk:

BERYL,

BE AT MAKINDU TOMORROW SEVEN AM STOP BRING WINSTON'S MAIL STOP CALL AT MANLEY'S AND COLLECT FIFTY ROUNDS AMMUNITION SIX BOTTLES GIN SIX BOTTLES PLASMA QUININE STOP MAKULA REPORTS HERD ELEPHANT WITH BIG BULL STOP BABU AT MAKINDU WILL SUPPLY WRITTEN DIRECTIONS FROM ME ON ARRIVAL STOP IF FISH DAY BRING FISH

BLIX

"Elephant! Safari! Hunting! I'll be there—fish and all!" Beryl exulted.

Winston Guest stood well over six foot and had the massive shoulders of an American football player. He was in fact a ten-goal polo player, as was his brother, Raymond. The product of a privileged background, he was brought up to aim for and expect the best. It would have to be the largest and heaviest-tusked elephant that Blix could find. Winston was due to arrive the following evening, and even if Blix scouted on foot in one direction, sending Makula and Simba in a second and third, they could only cover at the most fifteen miles in each direction.

The Kamba country, encircled by the Tiva River to the north and the Athi to the south, is one of dense, impenetrable bush. Wait-a-bit thorn and sansevieria stand guard to snag and ensnare. It is elephant country, and few men have need of it. Blix was one of the few.

As he sat looking across the table at the old Babu at Makindu, Blix wondered, as he watched him jab a finger in rhythmic code over the telegraph key, whether Beryl would make it. He had scribbled the directions, "Get to Kilamakoy. Look for smoke," with a graphic appendage of circles and arrows directed at the word "camp." It was lying there before him now, pinned together with other yellowing scraps, beneath a chipped mug. He waited for her answer.

Safari operations today are communicated by the indestructible and indiscreet radio telephone. Gone are the days when every station's Hindu "Babu" greeted you with a message or the offer to share his curry and spiced tea.

Awakened from his dreams by the sharp clatter of keys and the smiling face of the familiar Babu, Blix knew the answer. Hugging the Babu warmly, as though he alone had answered his cry for help, Blix flew out of the door and raced back to camp to tell Old Man Wicks the news and prepare the landing strip for Beryl.

Wicks managed a sugar estate near Masongaleni. Although he was barely forty, a monkish existence and constant malaria had reduced a youthful frame to skeletal proportions. Assisting Blix when he was in the area appeared to be his only diversion. Together they directed the porters in clearing a narrow strip.

The friendly drone of an engine could be heard long before Beryl's familiar Avian was spotted. Orders went out to light the fires. Old Man Wicks and Blix stood at each end, waving frantically.

As the plane waddled to a halt and the dust settled, Beryl

(Following page) *Blix chose his camps with great care and was particular about arranging for a landing strip nearby. Diana Guest Manning recalls, on a family safari, how Blix became anxious one night for Raymond who was supposed to have landed with Beryl Markham during the day. He took two scouts and kerosene lamps and walked the twenty-five miles to the nearest telegraph station in the middle of the night to make sure all was well (which it was) and returned at dawn in time to take his guests hunting.*

VP-K

stepped out, shaking her blond hair from the confines of her flying helmet.

"Is it me or Doctor Turvey you were expecting?"

"Both," smiled Blix, pointing to the bony figure beside him. "And this is Old Man Wicks."

A thimbleful of "Dr. Turvey's" prescribed panacea, a colorless liquid smelling unerringly of juniper, never failed to hit the spot. A bottle numbs the senses. No one ever saw Dr. Turvey, in whose telepathic diagnosis Blix had such confidence. "His very absence," explained Blix, "was bedside manner carried to perfection."

The Wakamba scouts had reported a large herd some way east of camp. Half an hour after landing, the Avian took off in that direction. The country stretched below, sometimes flat, sometimes hilly, like a child's painting daubed with ochre yellow, broken here and there by an awkward-limbed baobab and the spindle of game trails haphazardly drawn in.

Spotting elephant is very difficult. To the unaccustomed eye, the elephants are as one with anthills and rock outcrops, until suddenly the familiar form leaps out of the picture. Once they reveal themselves, you wonder why you did not see them in the first place.

No sooner had the herd come into focus when its flattened perspective moved as one beneath the Avian, ears swept forward in anger at the intrusion of such an ungainly and noisy bird. Beryl circled around, coming in low, while Blix pressed his nose to the window, eyes skinned for the big tusker among them. He hastily scribbled, "Look! The bull is enormous. Turn back. Doctor Turvey radios I should have some gin," and handed the note to Beryl over her shoulder. She nodded with a knowing look, turned to the controls, and banked around toward camp.

On the way back, Blix spotted four lone bulls a few miles out from camp. Three of them looked as though they were carrying big ivory. It didn't really seem fair that they should be within such easy reach, but it certainly made his job easier. There would be time to look them over on foot before Winston arrived.

After downing a slug of Dr. Turvey's elixir, they gathered up Makula and Simba. The four of them set off, with Makula in the lead, dressed as usual in a faded shuka, his torso bare except for the leather strap that held his quiver of poisoned arrows. He carried a long bow loosely in his right hand. The sun was high, with not a breath of wind. The procession moved forward in silence, each person aware only of the one in front—until the moment Makula stopped, ears cocked.

Hooking a finger over his shoulder to attract Blix's attention, Makula pointed to the wrinkled backs of two bulls, heads hidden in the bush. They had neither heard nor scented. He and Simba then disappeared with a backward shrug, as if to say "They're all yours, Bwana!"

Blix picked up a handful of dirt and let it out slowly between his fingers to assess the direction of the wind. Turning to Beryl, he signaled, "Watch the wind. We'll move round them. I want to see the tusks."

Negotiating a semicircle within hearing and seeing distance is no easy task. It is an infinitely slow process. Crouched low, each step is gingerly maneuvered, lifting heel and then toe, to lower toe and then heel. The mouth dries. The breath is caught in the throat. Stop. A twig cracks. Silence. A belly rumbles. An elephant's belly. Tread softly. Heel, toe, shaking ankle, toe, heel.

An hour eased out painfully, over a bare fifty yards, brought them around to face two heads rather than rumps. One-hundred pounders! Blix was satisfied and began to back off.

No sooner had his thoughts turned to a relaxed afternoon in camp than the nearest of the two bulls, trunk raised to test the air, swung around. He must have browsed over previous tracks and caught the scent. His ears, normally flapping idly like banana leaves, now spread out erect into two saucer-shaped direction finders. Blix pointed a finger earthwards and Beryl dropped down. Crawling on their stomachs, hoping to resemble some insignificant warthog, they slowly inched sideways. Focusing their eyes at two inches from the ground brought every miniscule ant and beetle into sharp relief, an unreal image in the haze of disjointed thought and fear of facing five tons of angry elephant. Surely he must see. He was so close. Blix stopped, the muscles of his back and neck strained taut to peer over the bush. Ten feet away! He stood up slowly and readied the gun. Beryl did likewise, clinging to his waist, eyes shut. She had ceased to breathe. Suddenly, that motionless mastodon swayed, threw his head high, and screamed, a chill, high-pitched scream that sent icy waves coursing down to the pit of the stomach. "He must shoot now," Beryl thought in fear.

Instead, Blix unleashed a series of gutter invectives. It only brought the elephant closer.

"I may have to shoot him," he said sadly.

"Oh God," thought Beryl, "that must be an understatement of classic magnificence."

The elephant screamed again. This time the chilling effect awakened his drowsy mates to the urgency of his alarm. They took off, tearing up the undergrowth as they fled. The remaining threat gave one last toss of his head and turned to join them in flight. Although the drama had unfolded over the space of only a few minutes, the relief brought at its ending seemed to bury it all as though it had never happened.

The shadows had lengthened. Sipping their drinks around the fire, Beryl turned to Blix and said, "I think you're the best hunter in Africa, but there are times when your humor goes too far. Why in hell didn't you shoot?"

"Come on, Beryl. You know as well as I do why. Those elephant are for Winston Guest."

"But what if he had charged?"

Blix extracted a beetle swimming drunkenly in his glass and said, "There's an old adage translated from the ancient Coptic that contains all the wisdom of the ages: Life is life and fun is fun, but it's all so quiet when the goldfish die!"

He was in fact an experienced enough hunter to know the difference between a mock charge and a real charge. When an elephant intentionally charges, he neither screams nor bellows but comes forward, head bowed, almost on his knees, swiftly and silently. That is why Blix did not shoot.

Within a day of arriving, Winston collected his "goldfish." Its tusks, though large, did not quite meet the penultimate round figure of one hundred pounds. He was a good shot and a sporting hunter. He aimed to collect the trophy of trophies. The cost of pursuing that record trophy, minus license fee, was today's equivalent of $600 per day—only half of what the charge is nowadays. A hundred-pounder was not impossible to find, but it was rare. Today it would be like stumbling on a gold bar on the Champs Elysées.

Between a flattened expanse of volcanic rock pitted with the dreaded spikes of sansevieria and stunted thorn whose branches weave an entangled web ankle high, emerge rocky pimples and hills a couple of hundred feet high. Apart from the luxury of soaring above it all in Beryl's machine, the only other alternative of extending the angle of vision was to climb a tree or a hilltop.

Principally in search of camp meat, the hunting party left camp just as the sky broke into a myriad of tinted streaks. The chill night air was still capable of raising goose pimples under a thin covering of bush khaki as Blix's line of followers wound their way toward the day's vantage point, a small rocky ridge a couple of miles from camp. By the time they reached the summit, the morning breezes were already beginning to dissipate as the sun's rays touched on faces and backs, a warning of the day's heat still to come.

Makula and Simba took off along the ridge while Blix took up the middle stand with Winston and Beryl, who was glad of the enforced rest, unused as she was to this awkward and slow method of getting about. The distance covered since dawn seemed pathetic now, viewed from above, in the waves of shimmering heat.

Simba saw them first. Whistling and clicking his tongue in imitation of a bird, he stabbed the air in the direction of a small herd of elephant caught napping on the edge of an open glade, their huge ochre-stained bodies barely visible among the gray expanse of thorn and bulbous euphorbia. They appeared to be all bulls, and only a mile distant.

With a signal from Blix, the others fell into line, descending the hill on the other side at speed, heedless of encumbering vegetation. Blix was almost running, stooping and side-stepping one moment, stretching the length of his body the next to peer over and through bush. He stopped so suddenly that Winston, swept forward by the momentum of the chase, thudded into his back.

Memories were still too recent for Beryl, who lagged behind a few paces, reluctantly closing the distance by hiding herself firmly behind Winston's powerful frame. Makula and Simba joined Blix at the front, then noiselessly moved out on either side to extend the field of vision. As one bull after another crossed in front of them, they could only stare unprepared and open-mouthed at a sight few people ever, and now never, see in a lifetime. Not one hundred-pounder, but two. No, three. God! They're all hundred-pounders and more. A life of poaching had never brought Makula within range of such booty. Even he was moved.

Imperceptibly, the wind veered. With a crescendo of stampeding feet and shrill trumpets of alarm, the entire herd moved off, mutilating and crushing trees and vegetation in their wake.

No one moved, each rooted in a trance set off by the vi-

Even though Blix did not shoot nearly as many elephants as the legendary "Karamoja" Bell, he was considered by many to be just as good a shot.

sion's sheer magnificence. There followed no recriminations, excuses, or regrets. The exhilaration of experiencing such a sight outweighed any disappointment Winston Guest might have felt in not realizing the hunter's dream. The sight would for all of them remain a memory forever.

Perhaps he did feel a slight twinge of disappointment at the unsuppressed excitement on learning of a lone bull elephant some fifteen miles away on the Yatta Plateau. "Let's go. What are we waiting for?" A dozen porters were organized into packing and carrying light fly tents, sleeping gear, and enough food to see them through two days. Blix planned to spend that night on the Athi, hunt the Yatta the following day, and with luck drop down the other side to cross the Tiva with the tusks, making for Ithumba on the third day at the latest. Arap Ruta and Farah, Blix's personal servant, would help Old Man Wicks take the lorries the long way around to set up base camp at Ithumba.

He and Winston saw Beryl off to Nyeri, where she was to stay a couple of days with John and June Carberry while the Avian was serviced.

"Don't let that joker J.C. fleece you! We need you at Ithumba in three days' time."

Beryl laughed as she adjusted the strap of her helmet. "J.C.'s all right—just a morbid sense of humor."

She started the engine, turned the aeroplane, and took off, leaving Blix and Winston ahead of their motley crew of porters to be swallowed up by the bush.

Drugged by the lulling sound of water and the seeping warmth of Dr. Turvey's tonic, the two men bedded down early to the murmured chattering of porters squatted down beside the fire a few yards distant.

The morning brought hope for the hunt and a steaming cup of sweetened tea, noisily deposited by Simba. Blix told him to take the men onto the plateau and wait for him there. He, Winston, and the birdlike Makula set off at a fast pace to get to the top as it got light.

By midday, not even the panicked flight of an alarmed bird had broken the riddle. No spoor. No tracks. No elephant.

"It looks as though the old boy's got the wind of us."

"Well, I guess there's always tomorrow," said Winston hopefully, as he stirred the fire with a stick.

"Trouble is, we didn't bring much food and the boys will be left short. If we haven't caught up with him by midday, we'd better pack it in and make for Ithumba as planned. We can always come back reprovisioned."

"Here's to tomorrow!" said Winston, raising his glass.

Blix awoke early and sleepily tugged on a pair of crumpled trousers before going outside to pee and glass the horizon. He was unprepared for what he saw. The plateau was marooned. The rising waters of the Tiva and the Athi surrounded it on either side. Rains, unseen and unheard, had fallen in the night far to the west and had transformed a turgid flow into a runaway flood, uprooting and plundering its banks as it raced toward the sea.

"Winston!" shouted Blix. "Take a look at this. Your elephant has probably crossed the Tiva by now, leaving you and me up here like fools chasing a ghost."

"Perhaps we could give it another try this morning while the boys clear a landing strip," replied Winston.

Before Blix could answer, Simba sided up to tap him on the shoulder and announced a small matter concerning the porters and the probable lack of food. Judging by the look on Blix's face and the language that followed, Winston guessed the matter was obviously no "Shauri kidogo"—no small matter.

"Goddam it!" Blix exploded, "They won't work without posho [maize meal]. How do they expect to get off the damn place without stirring their bloody arses?"

"That leaves you and me, does it?" said Winston carefully.

"Damn right! Forget the elephant, Winston. Let's go over and talk to them."

A circle of sullen faces met them. Makula had diplomatically seated himself some way off where he was busily

(Following page) *The baobab tree gives the impression of having been planted upside down with its roots pointing heavenward. In reality it's a tree benefiting men as well as beast. The enormous trunk stores precious water reserves, the bark (which the elephants unfortunately have discovered) contains many important nutrients. The gnarled branches and their hollows provide protection and shelter for a multitude of birds and smaller warm-blooded animals.*

paring an arrow head, pretending he had nothing to do with this unruly bunch of strikers. Rational argument proved futile. No food, no work.

The top of the Yatta is stony, but well covered in primeval scrub thorn. To their advantage, it is at least flat. But the wherewithal to clear the growth consisted of a couple of pangas, that all-purpose tool common to Africa for cutting, slashing, digging, and stirring. Clearing a hundred-yard strip in that melee of tangled weed was not unlike using a kitchen knife on a garden overgrown with brambles. Simba elected to join the workers. Like men possessed, they spat into the palms of their hands, took a firm grip of the panga, and unleashed a pent-up fury against those that lolled and idled in a firm belief that the Lord would provide.

By the third day, the clearing began to look, at least from the ground, somewhat like an airstrip. They suspected that from the air it looked like a walled-in cabbage patch. Simba set fire to the piles of wood and brush set aside at each end. The wood, still green and blessed with a capacity to withstand drought, refused to burn easily. After a lot of coaxing and swearing, it finally sputtered to life and emitted a dreary, pale gray smoke signal.

The Avian droned overhead at around midday. Winston and Blix waved hats furiously in the air, willing Beryl to come in. She flew so low they could almost reach out and touch her. But far short of landing, the aeroplane pulled up and away.

"Come on girl! *Land!*" thought Blix.

As if in answer to his prayer, the plane circled around again and dropped a small beribboned package. It floated down effortlessly and fetched up in a wall of bush beside them.

> Might get down but runway looks too short for take-off. Will return later if you can make it longer.

"Oh boy, oh boy," said Winston, throwing his hat petulantly on the ground. "Can't she see there are just the three of us?"

His dejection was premature, for the little plane returned immediately, taking a course straight to them, to land bumping and swaying like a drunken wagtail to the very edge of the clearing.

"I hated to ask you to land, but I had to. There's no way we could have extended the runway another foot," said Blix, helping Beryl down. Adding, as he hugged her, "Besides, I knew you'd make it."

"Thank God, you got here!" said Winston.

Looking at them, disheveled and unshaven, she replied, "I'm not sure I have come to the right place. Both of you look like total strangers."

"We'll explain later," said Blix. "Did you bring anything?"

"What, something to eat? No, afraid not. Didn't you manage to shoot something?"

"Not a thing. We haven't eaten for three days, Beryl. I was thinking, though, more along the lines of something wet."

"Well," mused Beryl, "perhaps. As a matter of fact I do have something hidden in the locker. J.C. gave it to me for Old Man Wicks. I'm sure he won't mind you having a swig."

Poor Old Wicks never got the opportunity to prove his largesse or have a taste of his own gin. Like an invisible pendulum, the bottle swung between the men until the last drop had been drained. After handing Blix the bottle for the last time, Winston wiped his mouth with the back of his hand and climbed into the front of the Avian, where he chose to remain silent until they were at least airborne. Blix swung the propellor and watched, breath held, while the plane once more scattered dust, its wheels fighting to gain a grip, before taking off to regain a dignified balance in the sky.

Beryl returned later in the day with enough posho and beans for the porters to see them through for a week. Simba elected to stay with them so they wouldn't feel Blix had abandoned them. Makula reluctantly agreed to fly, sitting bolt upright blinded in the folds of his shuka, which he had wrapped completely around him.

The safari over, Winston and Beryl returned to mundane living. Beryl went back to a scheduled flying pattern, he to America and the world of big business.

Blix was never sure how he fitted in. No hunting day was ever the same, and in between safaris the days were lived out with friends, never alone. He no longer cared to return to Babati. Essentially gregarious, he loved people and parties. Up-country hospitality would not have failed him: "Do come to dinner. We've got Bror coming to stay." Or, "Blix! This is a surprise! Let's have a party. It's been so long."

He would often stay with my parents on their coffee farm, Samuru, some thirty miles outside Nairobi at Thika, where much of his mail would be addressed. My father remembers leaving him with a huge batch of envelopes and bills after a fairly long absence. Returning later to see if his guest needed anything by way of a drink, Father was surprised to see Blix had thrown a good proportion into the waste paper basket unopened.

"Hey, Blix. I see you've sorted the mail. What about this lot?" said Father, pointing to the overflowing waste.

Blix tiredly gathered up the few before him and replied, "These I must pay. The rest can go on the fire."

On Eva's return to Kenya at the end of 1933, Blix wangled an invitation for her to join a trip with American

Blix, here tending to Eva Dickson, seldom was caught short by the demands of safari.

Shooting animals to use their skins for shoes and handbags for personal use was a popular sport among the safari women of the day.

ornithologists to Lake Baringo. The lake is one of a string of fresh-water lakes on the floor of the Rift Valley. Dotted with small islands and reedy river inlets, it has an abundance of bird life. Rose Cartwright, whose knowledge of birds was greater than Blix's, assisted him on the trip. As Geoffrey Buxton's sister, she was herself a competent hunter and accompanied Blix as second hunter on many occasions. She shot a record-book Bongo antelope, which is still, today, one of the biggest ever shot. A great admirer of Blix, she considered him one of her best friends and a first-class hunter. "An excellent shot, a meticulous organiser, and very good teacher. He was on a par with the best African trackers, and they admired him greatly for his skills and stamina."

George Vanderbilt, Alfred's brother, organized a similar trip two years later with a group from the Philadelphia Museum and his friend from France, Sosthenes de la Rochefaucauld. Blix took them into Uganda via Entebbe and Butiaba, to Wamba in the Belgian Congo, and through what was then the German Cameroon to Kribi on the Atlantic coast, nearly losing George at the outset to a crocodile on Lake Victoria.

Returning to camp one evening from checking the nets, George beached the boat, stepped glibly ashore, and arrived in camp slightly non-plussed at being pursued by a wild-eyed and breathless native fisherman. "The boat, Bwana—eaten by a crocodile."

"But that's impossible," he told Blix after a pause for translation, "I've only just come from there."

As the man gesticulated and wrung his hands Blix explained, "He was surprised you didn't see the croc. Apparently he came out of the water just seconds behind you. I suggest we go down and have a look."

When they got to the lake edge, sure enough, bits of rubber boat were scattered in all directions. Watching George's approach, the crocodile's conditioned thinking had been thwarted on finding an empty plate, and the subsequent destruction must have resulted out of its angry frustration.

At Butiaba, the governor gave them the loan of his boat, manned by ten oarsmen. For nearly one hundred miles across Lake Albert and down the Nile, they traveled to the rhythmic singing of the oarsmen as they splashed and dipped the oars. During this lilting serenade, the boat hugged the shore, stopping at places of historical interest, villages, or just simply to stretch a leg, view game, eat, or sleep. Their course was a far cry from that taken by the bearded explorers, Speke, Baker, and Livingston, some eighty years before.

The expedition hoped to record and capture on movie film the undisturbed behavior pattern of a group of elephants: "A Day in the Life of an Elephant." Each member of the herd was given a name. The leader, a single-toothed, wizened gentleman of some years' standing, was named One Tusk. To the others Blix accorded names of past friends and lovers; Eva, George, Cockie, Charles. George behaved like a difficult teenager whose entry into the ranks of men is attained with unseemly aggression and bravado. He must have overstepped the limit, for One Tusk saw him out of the herd with a deafening trumpet call. George sulked for a while some way off before slowly returning, placing his trunk alongside the leader's as if to say, "I'm sorry. I'll try to be better behaved next time." One Tusk accepted the apology by patting the young bull's head with his trunk and leading him back into the fold.

The scientific venture completed, the safari moved back to Kenya for a fun few weeks. There, they were joined by George Vanderbilt's mother.

It was probably the most expensive safari ever outfitted. A fleet of twenty trucks carried equipment and stores, which included cases of champagne (champagne took preference because wine, shipped, did not travel well) and tentage to accommodate the guests and their organizers. These included Philip Percival as co-hunter; Ben Fourie, assistant hunter; the pilot of the Waco aircraft, Wood; camp managers Donald Ker and Blix's nephew Romolus; the mechanic, Jack Harris; and Blix's major domo, Farah Aden, to supervise the mess. No one ever went to bed before two in the morning, leaving the organizers little time to plan amusements for the following day. The entire camp was moved every few days. While camp broke up, the guests spent the day hunting or sightseeing. When they returned in the evening, Wood shuttled them to the new site, where a landing strip had been prepared and the tents erected. The plane left each day for Nairobi, either to take a guest to the hairdresser or trophies to Zimmerman, the taxidermist. It brought back fresh supplies, including fish and Evian water for the Vanderbilt matriarch's bath.

Blix was by now becoming more and more interested in photography. "These days I prefer to hunt with a camera. A good photograph demands more skill from the hunter, better nerves and more patience than a rifle shot," Blix told my father.

Of course then, without the benefit of powerful telephoto lenses, game photography did require infinite patience. The hunter, encumbered with a large black box and tripod, had to stalk his subject and position himself closer than is needed today. If his nerves weren't steady, the camera wasn't either. You could afford to take a bad photograph, but not a bad shot. The hunter is both observer and naturalist. He puts himself on the same footing as his prey. He has a far greater understanding of wildlife and its complex make-up than the stay-at-home scientist or conservationist.

Being out in the bush so much, Blix found himself befriending the odd orphaned or stray animal. His two favorite wild pets were a buffalo calf called Lotti, after his first girlfriend in Sweden, and a lion cub called Hans, after his brother. He had found Lotti abandoned on the plain, wobbling uneasily on new-born legs. He hand reared her, and she grew up into a tough little black bovine. She took on the role

(Following page) *Eva was a skilled hunter and during her relatively short time in East Africa she felled a number of large antelope, buffalo, and rhino.*

of watchdog, following Blix's heels by day and by night planting herself squarely in the triangle of his tent, daring anyone to enter. Before she was quite full grown, she died of the tick-borne disease, East Coast fever, the bane of stock breeders.

Hans had been brought to him during a spell as timber hauler up-country in the 1920s when Blix had found himself broke. As mischievous as any kitten, Hans delighted in tearing paper to shreds, a habit that usually ended in a spanking, for any available paper was more than likely the rare once-weekly newspaper. He strode fearlessly among the oxen and the men sawing, but would race back to Blix every time the steam whistle blew. At six months, he grew too large to share the bed, and it was always Blix who found himself sleeping on the floor. Eventually the call of the wild beckoned and Hans left.

With the Vanderbilt safari over, Blix flew to America with Dick Cooper, and they met up again with Eva. The three of them traveled to Palm Beach to stay with Ernest Hemingway, whom Blix had known during the years of hunting with Philip Percival. The two men were similar. They lived physically: hunting, fishing, drinking, and womanizing. Most of the stay was spent fishing on Hemingway's boat *Pilar* and on the Bimini Island in the Bahamas. Leaving the warm south, the three of them returned to New York and the lavish Vanderbilt hospitality. No official record of a marriage has ever come to light, but Eva returned from New York as the third Baroness von Blixen.

The year 1935 was rounded off with a trip to Abyssinia, or Ethiopia, with a view to looking at new hunting country. Blix and Eva were warmly received by the emperor himself and stayed in the palace overlooking the beginnings of a large and sprawling city of mud houses, Addis Ababa. Haile Selassie was believed to be a direct descendant of King Solomon and the Queen of Sheba. His normally easy manner was however distracted with the threat of Benito Mussolini's troops

Blix and Eva

marching on the capital. Troops were already in position at Adowa with that intention and were determined not to repeat the failure of their defeat there in 1895. Haile Selassie prepared to escape into exile, leaving Blix and Eva to retreat as best they could. The country was virtually at war, with no transport available except two mules, on whose sturdy backs they rode a slow boat home to Kenya.

Having arranged to fly to England with Beryl in her Leopard Moth later in 1936, Blix booked no professional safari for the beginning of the year. With time on his hands, he took out his cousin Nils Frijs.

The evening before departure was celebrated with a dinner

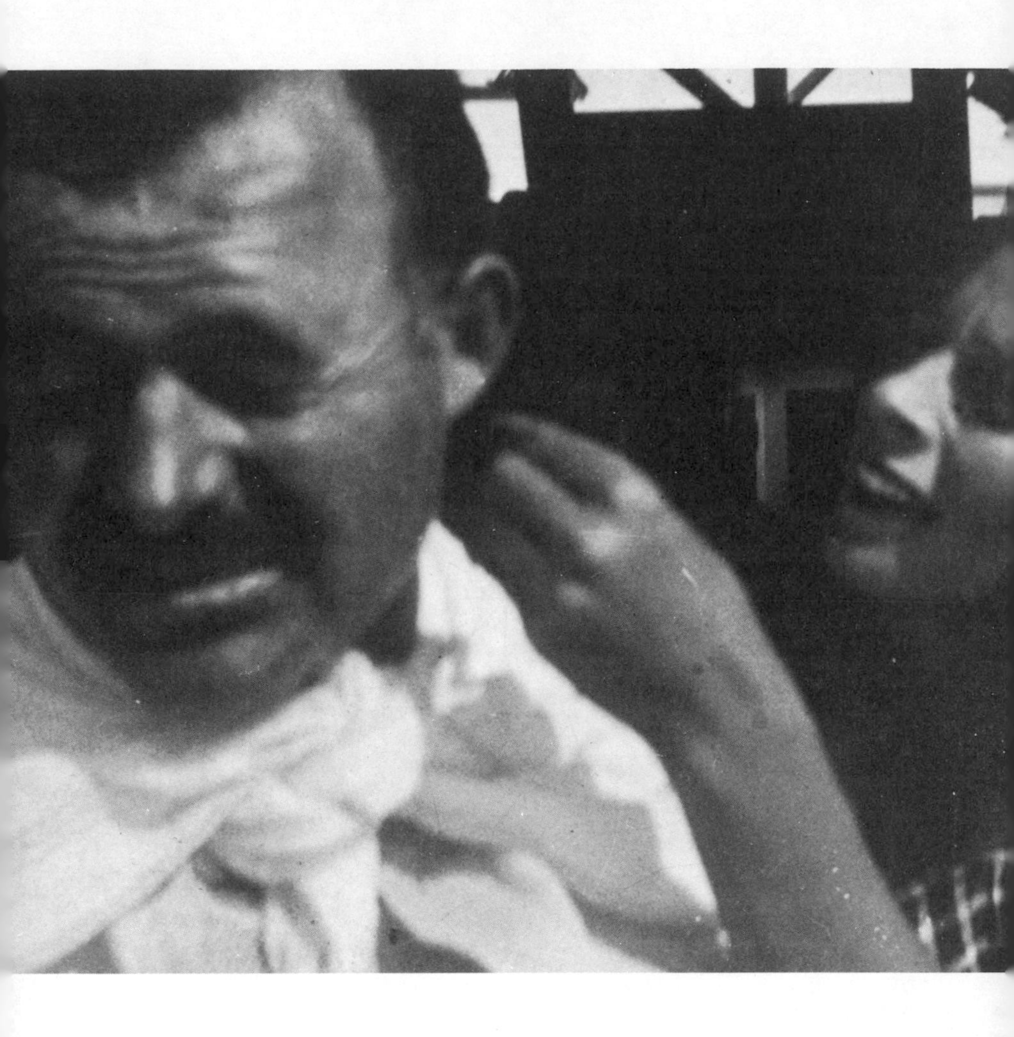

In May 1935 Blix and Eva went to Miami to visit Ernest Hemingway. They stayed onboard Hemingway's yacht, **Pilar.** *During their visit Hemingway turned out to be obviously proud of Blix's presence and constantly engaged him in conversations about Africa and big game hunting. Other guests, including his old fishing companion Strater, were kindly but firmly excluded from these conversations.*

party at the Club. Among those invited were my grandparents (Count and Countess Bonde) and the beautiful heiress Barbara Hutton, then married to the Dane, Count Reventlow. My grandfather always enjoyed a good thrash but tended to become confused as the evening wore on. Suddenly, enthusiastically taking events into his own hands, he stood up, turned to Barbara Hutton, and with raised glass thanked her on behalf of himself and those present for a generous hospitality and a delightful evening. Court Frijs, the actual host, was extremely annoyed.

The following month, Blix again took out family. This time he included my grandfather, his cousin Nils Bonde, and my parents on a hunt in the Serengeti. Eva, the restless wanderer, was in Sweden hoping, even demanding, to be taken on as a war correspondent to cover the Ethiopian campaign. Her absence didn't worry Blix, who was a firm believer in letting events take their course. Besides, Nils Bonde's daughter Brita was also on the safari, a most decorative young girl.

It was on this family safari that my father narrowly escaped laceration, or worse, at the hands of a leopard. He was then just beginning a career himself as a White Hunter and with Blix had been following the tracks of a leopard, considered vermin in those days, along the bottom of a dry river bed. The tracks led into a compact thicket, so they circled it, looking for possible outgoing spoor.

Without warning, a leopard sprang out. Father shot, breaking the cat's momentum, and hurriedly reloaded. Blix shouted: "Look out! He's coming."

Father had his eyes peeled on the animal thrashing on the ground before him and did not see a second threat launched to the side and behind him.

Reflexively, Blix swung his rifle like a shotgun and, with no time to take aim, fired. The bullet miraculously broke the cat's neck in mid-flight, bringing an end to 150 pounds of spotted fury.

"Thank God! Where the hell did *he* come from?"

"You were lucky there, Krister," answered Blix, pointing to the spot. "I thought for a moment one of us would end up with a squeaky voice."

Safaris behind him for the time being, Blix, never one for overburdening life with possessions, was armed with no more than a small suitcase and a tissue-wrapped bottle cradled lovingly in the crook of his arm as he waited for Beryl on the apron. The skies were overcast, laden with the promise of rain. He was just beginning to wonder if she'd make it when Beryl bumped down the runway toward him. Arap Ruta was with her. It would be his last flight, for they would not see each other for a very long time.

"Ready?"

"Ready. You won't mind if I go to sleep. Had rather a bad night last night."

"I know," smiled Beryl. "A night lived as though it were your last. You've no faith in your old friend, I see."

Blix climbed in, leaving Beryl the privacy of a last farewell to Arap Ruta. When she got in, he could see in her set expression a determination not to cry. They traveled to Juba in silence, Beryl with her thoughts, Blix with his dreams.

Between Juba on the Nile and Khartoum in the north lies hundreds of miles of primeval swamp, uninhabited and uninhabitable. The sudd is a miasma of stinking weed and papyrus six feet high, cover to the ghosts of prehistoric pachiderms whose diminutive, scaly descendants slide beneath the swamp's stagnant waters and muddy sludge waiting for a hapless migratory bird to drop down, exhausted.

"Do you remember Ernst Udet?" said Beryl, breaking the silence.

"Mm," acknowledged Blix sleepily. "Shot a buffalo with me in Tanganyika."

"He went down somewhere here. Ran out of petrol. Tom Black rescued them eventually, half eaten by mosquitos.

Udet and his mechanic had had nothing to eat for five days. The mosquitos were so bad they were unable to sleep or even make a fire. Tom told me he arrived just in time, for Udet had planned to shoot the mechanic and then himself rather than die ignominiously of starvation."

"You tell me *now,*" said Blix. "In that case, don't wake me up until we get to Khartoum."

Sterile desert gradually took over. Khartoum lies well north, a city of impoverished houses shut off and darkened from the desert glare and frequent sandstorms. The water, tepid and brackish, could be improved with a splash of whiskey, but there was plenty of it to get cleaned up and feel human again.

They were met the following day in Cairo by customs. The gray-suited Abdullah Ali had witnessed Beryl's passage through his official domain on previous occasions and greeted her like a long-lost friend.

"Is that all?" he said pointing to Blix's small suitcase. The fringe on his red fez swung violently at each energetic stamp on passport and luggage.

Beryl held out her hand expectantly.

"Orders!" barked Abdullah, pinning the passports under the flat of his palm. "The Italians, you understand," he continued more kindly, "insist you get permission from them to overfly Libya."

"The Italians! How long will that take?"

"Ah that, my friends," replied Abdullah, shrugging his shoulders, "could take forever."

"In that case," suggested Blix, "we might as well make ourselves comfortable at Shepheard's."

Beryl's only highly placed contact had made himself scarce. There was nothing to do but wait and fill the time patiently telephoning, visiting, pleading, imploring, and still managing a smile as they were shown the door once more. At the close of each day, the reply was always the same. Frustration mounted. Blix went out and got drunk. At least he got those around him drunk, felling each drinking companion in turn while, to all outward appearances, he himself remained perfectly sober.

Cairo nightlife under King Farouk catered to every taste and perversion. To lose oneself in its warren of dens and brothels was akin to a glimpse of Hell. Blix was not easily shocked or shockable, but walking back to Shepheard's Hotel in the early hours of the morning, he was unprepared to stumble on a severed head rolling leadenly at his feet. Looking up from its sightless eyes, he noticed a small crowd gathered chattering and arguing over the head's lifeless companion. He picked up the bloodied head by a tuft of hair and carried it over, still dripping. The group parted, angry voices silenced. Blix gently joined the head to the body and ran back to the hotel.

Permission to fly over Libya finally arrived. Beryl took off to land, as instructed, at Amseat on the Egyptian-Italian (Libyan) border. No sooner had the plane settled when a phalanx of roaring motor bikes rode in and surrounded it. Communication between Amseat and Cairo had not provided for *carte-blanche* to Europe. Papers were confiscated and hurried away to some nebulous authority. Eager hands dissected the contents of the aeroplane. God knows what they expected to find! Even Beryl's feminine cool failed to penetrate Latin blood on the military boil. A neat pile of cigarette stubs, inhaled over a three-hour wait in the boiling sun, stood half buried in the sand as a monument to patience.

"You may now proceed to Benghazi. You do not fly by way of Tobruk and the coast."

"But there is no desert route."

Jabbing a finger at a cross on the map the captain continued, "You will fly here to this fort and then around it three times. Then to this one and to this one. Is that clear? If you do not, you will be arrested in Benghazi. Now you may go."

Instructions completed, the motor bikes gunned into action and withdrew. Beryl and Blix were thankful to be airborne.

The first fort was not easy to find, camouflaged as it was in the desert. When they did eventually spot it, Beryl dutifully circled three times. The second fort came into view soon afterward, and the third never materialized. Afraid of running short of fuel, they decided to risk arrest and head straight for Benghazi, which they only just made before nightfall.

Every hotel room was occupied.

"Take us anywhere so long as there's a bed." said Blix to the driver, who had already run up a fortune in fares driving the roundabout route from hotel to hotel, with the full knowledge that every spare niche had been commandeered by Il Duce's boys.

The car idled to a stop in front of a shabby, two-story mud building with one light, giving it the appearance of a blind begger winking in the night.

"You are fortunate, no?" said the man.

Looking up at the broken windows stuffed with old rags, Blix wondered just how fortunate. At one end of a dim courtyard festooned with faded washing they were met by the lonely, wasted figure of a woman shuffling in on slippered feet. Her heavily made-up face clouded on the realization that all they wanted was a bed. By the worn expression and clothes that hung limply over her sagging bosoms, Blix judged that customers had been scarce lately. She led them up the stairs by the light of a candle and showed them their rooms, bare except for an iron spring bed, a torn and stained mattress, and a pillow. A wash basin stood on the floor in one, and its jug on the floor of the other. Neither held water. Blix gestured, implying a wish for food and drink. The woman beckoned. He followed her to a cockroach-infested kitchen, where he found the odd tin or two. As he pried them open, Blix attempted to engage the woman in conversation in as many languages as he could muster. Dutch appeared to be a common ground. Haltingly, her sad and sordid tale came out.

She had been kidnapped at the age of seven and shipped to Africa, where she had been sold into slavery. She remembered nothing of her own country except that it might have been Holland. This notion, and the language, had been picked up at the hands of a Dutch sailor who had probably been kinder to her than most. She hoped to return there, but had no money. Blix too was short, for he had lost most of what he possessed in a barber's shop in Cairo. A little, although not enough to see her back, might at least serve to brighten an impoverished existence and provide a rare glimmer of hope.

Leaving Benghazi and its brothel behind, they flew over the dense waters of the Gulf of Sidra to Tripoli and Tunis, their last glimpse of Africa before embracing the Mediterranean and Europe.

A white-out and violent winds hit them over Sardinia. Beryl coaxed the plane higher and higher, until clear blue skies opened out at 10,000 feet. Blix unquestioningly put his faith in her hands and promptly fell asleep, to be awakened just before touchdown in Cannes. They refueled the plane before flying on to Paris. There they stayed the night, celebrating at the Ritz with old friends Ernest Hemingway, who had just flown in from the Spanish Civil War, and Sosthenes de la Rochfaucauld.

Blix's relationship with Eva was confusing to the outsider, to say the least, a mercurial bond that was satisfactory to neither.

"How can you let Eva Dickson call herself Baroness Blixen?" someone asked Blix.

"If it amuses her, let her do so," was his reply.

Eva's brother Ake was in the publishing business and suggested Blix write a book about his years in Africa. He sent

Beryl was also expected to have a brilliant career as a horse trainer, and was in fact the leading trainer in Kenya, and later South Africa, for a number of years.

Blix and an editor alone to a small island in the Stockholm Archipelago, where, after a month of late nights and heavy drinking, Blix's first book, *Nyama,* was conceived. The editor, until then a moderate drinker, returned to the mainland a wreck.

Blix then flew to England to get photographs of his trip with the Prince of Wales, then King Edward. He planned to meet up again with Eva.

Eva, in the meantime, had decided to compete with Beryl in an "if she can so can I" attitude: she agreed to navigate for a Swedish aviator, Bjorkwall, on an Atlantic flight from New York to Gothenburg. In July she boarded the Zeppelin *Hindenburg* at Frankfurt, landing five days later at Lakehurst, New Jersey. From contemporary newspaper cuttings, her arrival, arm in arm with the millionaire playboy Thomas Hamilton, caused quite a stir. Hamilton distracted her vision to navigate, and then in turn dropped her for another beauty. Eva ended up in New York companionless and rather broke. She returned to Sweden later in the year for a reunion with Blix, but was still undecided about whether to join him permanently in Africa.

Meanwhile, Beryl was preparing herself for the challenge of a lifetime: an Atlantic flight, single-handed, from East to West. She was the first, man or woman, to do so from England. (Jim Mollison achieved it from Ireland.) Her Kenya friend, John "J.C." Carberry, agreed to back her in financing the aeroplane, a Vega Gull made for her by Edward Percival at his factory at Gravesend. September was not the most auspicious month to have chosen for flying blind at night over an immense stretch of black water, without benefit of a radio. Bad weather drove her too far north. Ice lodged in the air intake of the last fuel tank, partially choking the fuel flow to the carburetor. While heading south again toward Stanley Airport, where she hoped to refuel before the last leg to New York, the engine cut out and she was forced to land in a bog just short of Sydney in Nova Scotia. Although she did not

At her arrival in New York, Beryl was properly and deservedly honored. One person who was especially impressed was the American flying ace Rickenbacker.

Beryl's heroic flights over the Atlantic resulted not only in honor and fame but also in a book that she wrote some years later, **West with the Night.** *In this book she describes her childhood and youth growing up in Kenya, her years as a horse trainer and her job as pilot for Blix, culminating in the flight over the Atlantic. It is one of the best books ever written about East Africa.*

make New York in her own plane, she had crossed the Atlantic in twenty-one hours and fifteen minutes.

Beryl subsequently wrote a book with the help of her journalist husband, Raoul Schumacher, *West with the Night.* Its publication coincided with the invasion of Pearl Harbor, and consequently it lay buried until 1983. It is, in my view, the most beautiful and evocative book ever written about Africa. Hemingway said of it: "She has written so well, and marvelously well, that I was completely ashamed of myself as a writer."

In the winter of 1937, Blix took out for Kenya safari Lord Furness, the shipping magnate; his wife, Enid; her two sons by a previous marriage, Pat and Caryll; and Lord Furness' daughter Avril. Enid Furness, an Australian by birth, was considered one of the most beautiful women of her time. She married five times, and each of her husbands died, leaving her a fortune. "Duke" Furness, as he was known, was Enid's second husband. For the winter, the Furnesses had a house in Muthaiga near the Club, appointed and decorated by Enid herself, who was famous for creating beautiful houses all over the world.

Into this household she brought a striking sixteen-year-old Swedish girl, Anne Boberg, to act as lady's maid, chaperone, and postman. Anne was initially introduced to the Furness' Leicestershire household as companion to the daughters. Anne was liked by them all, and particularly by Enid, who persuaded Duke to allow her to come out with them to Kenya. There she became Enid's unwitting accomplice, collecting and delivering letters at the Club—Lady Furness was not short of admirers. Anne was expected to accompany Enid to town in the guise of chaperone, where she would be told to "amuse herself until it was time to go home." Anne was often left alone, confused by her role as daughter of the house, guest, and errand girl.

Blix took her under his wing, calling her "my little

daughter." Realizing her need for company of her own age, he would steal her out of the house at night to drive her to whatever young party was in swing that evening. At a weekend party at the Lindstroms', she met Romolus Kleen, of whom she remembers, "Unbeknown to Romolus, I fell in love for the first time."

Of Blix she writes: "A more generous, kind, compassionate, unpretentious man God never created. There was hardly a woman who met him, who did not fall for him. Gregarious, he could party all night and still stand behind a paying client, never missing an elephant or charging Rhino!"

One of the Furness daughters ran off with a White Hunter. When permission to marry was turned down with the words "They can go to hell," the reply dropped into camp from an aeroplane, simply reading, "We have gone to heaven."

The Furnesses left Kenya, taking Anne with them, in Duke's new aeroplane, a Lockheed Electra piloted by Tom Black.

Shortly afterward, in the spring of 1937, Blix went to Europe and then America to attend Freddie Guest's funeral. He and Eva met up in Europe. She was again contemplating another driving adventure, this time across the Asian continent. Preparations were already underway with the help of Sven Hedin, the explorer, the last Swede to be knighted for his efforts. Eva promised that she would return to Africa with Blix when it was all over. However, it was never to be. The following year, she was killed in a car accident in India.

When Eva died, Cockie was then living in Johannesburg, married to an architect, Jan Hoogterp. The leading newspaper muddled the two Baronesses von Blixen, and the editor telephoned Cockie to apologize.

"Don't mention it," said Cockie. "I'm returning all my bills marked 'Deceased.'"

"No, no. I insist we correct the error in any words you care to choose."

"Any words?" responded Cockie.

"Certainly."

Cockie dictated over the telephone, and the newspaper printed: "Mrs. Hoogterp wishes it to be known that she has not yet been screwed into her coffin."

On his return to Africa, Blix felt unsettled. He was dispirited by Eva's death and disturbed by rumors of another European war. His last year in Africa was taken up going on safaris with old clients: Dick Cooper, Raymond and Winston Guest, Sosthenes de la Rochefaucauld, Graham Beech, and his family.

My mother remembers a day of bird shooting. Standing watching the others, she was leaning, propped against her gun, with one hand resting on the barrels. Blix walked over and slammed his fist down on her hand. "Don't ever let me see you do that again!" A bruised impression remained in the palm of her hand for weeks afterwards—a painful and effective reminder of how not to handle firearms.

On Blix's last safari, it seemed fitting that Romolus, his nephew, whom he had first introduced to Africa, should assist him on the last hunt with the Englishman Graham Beech.

In the 1930s, Romolus lived in a rented cottage in Muthaiga, near the Club, going into Nairobi each morning to his job with a land agency and coffee brokerage firm. Blix often stayed with his nephew, giving parties for clients and friends from the cottage.

One morning as Romolus was leaving for work, Blix said, "Romolus, I would like to give a party this evening for the clients and their friends."

"Sounds fun," agreed Romolus, gulping down still-scalding coffee.

"I thought we'd come on after the dancing at Torr's and bring the band with us."

"The band! Dear Uncle, there's barely enough room for the two of us!"

"True," said Blix. "We are a bit cramped. A small extension is needed. Yes, we could extend and enclose the veranda, and put a fireplace at one end."

Incredulous, Romolus thought it best not to argue, but he doubted his uncle was in his right mind.

On Romolus' return home that evening, he hardly recognized his own house. Blix had hired a bevy of stonemasons, carpenters, painters, and sewing girls. The extension was complete, down to the last curtain and cushion. Bottles of champagne lay cooling in a bath filled with ice. The party was so successful that Romolus was beseiged by letters from angry neighbors who had been kept awake.

Thereafter, to safeguard his nephew's reputation, Blix held his parties at Happy Marshall's. Before becoming a restaurateur, Happy Marshall had been the government hangman.

Like many others in Kenya during these lean years, Romolus and Blix lived on credit. Sometimes they stretched it to the limit and beyond, thus attracting the attention of a very energetic debt collector called Jimmy Price. This time it was Romolus he was giving a bit of a hard time. Romolus confided in his uncle and asked his advice. Blix told him, "Don't worry. I'll think of something."

Blix had just completed a safari with the Guest brothers on the Galana River and had left behind a fully provisioned camp in charge of his camp manager, who had stayed on to disassemble a broken wing from Winston Guest's aircraft. Blix suggested Romolus take a week off, giving as his excuse the need to show a prospective buyer the boundaries of a farm in Tanganyika. "Fatty" Pearson who, like Beryl, was doing the mail run between Wilson Airport and Mombasa, flew Romolus down to Lala Hill. Pearson had been instructed by Blix to circle over any big herds of elephant and to give Romolus a compass bearing and a head start. The plan worked beautifully. Four days later, Romolus had collected six tusks weighing around a hundred pounds apiece. Mr.

Price was delighted, and raised a glass to their success.

On the final hunt with Graham Beech, Blix decided to open up new country by cutting a track along the Voi River as far as the Mariakani-Lamu Road. As this was his last hunt, Blix aimed to shoot nothing less than a 120-pound tusker, and he made Romolus and Graham promise to do the same. After several uneventful weeks, Romolus and his tracker, Ngondo (Simba's brother), saw what seemed to them an enormous tusker. They agreed its body was small. But the tusks! They were large and thick. Surely this was the one they ought to shoot.

Romolus was beginning to regret his impetuosity as he neared camp. Blix was standing waiting. "You've broken your promise! Toothpicks!"

His anger was, however, short-lived. The tusks scaled a 105 and 110 pounds, and nothing more was shot on that trip.

Before Graham Beech's hunt was over, Romolus had to leave for Europe. Blix gave him a surprise farewell party at Mariakani Station, where he had organized friends and girlfriends to travel down from Nairobi. The party was disturbed halfway through by an invasion of safari ants, which had the guests scurrying around in various stages of undress in the glimmer of the only light available, the babu's single tilly lamp. Unused to the sight of so much bare flesh, the babu retired, shocked, to his quarters.

Blix had long been alarmed by a renewed German influence in Tanganyika. Germans, sponsored by the Hitler regime, were buying up land, banks, and business concerns. He instructed Romolus to see Winston Churchill in London, since he was the only political figure who understood the present position in Tanganyika. Romolus did not get an interview with Churchill, but saw Duff Cooper. Duff Cooper listened but was unreceptive. Anyway, more important issues soon emerged.

Blix's parting advice to Romolus, from an "experienced hand," was:

1. If you have to stay in a hotel, choose the best. The best give credit.
2. If you form a liaison with a woman, choose one who has her own business. This type, wary of her reputation, is not anxious to be seen with you in restaurants which you cannot afford.

Blix certainly had had experience of hotels. When in Copenhagen, he stayed at the Hotel d'Angleterre. Romolus remembers an occasion in 1938 on Blix's way to the United States when Mr. Haslev, the night porter there, greeted him on his return one evening:

> Baron, while you were away, Prince Axel left a message inviting you to dinner. I therefore took the liberty of sending a boy to your sister's house in Helsingborg for your dinner jacket, which is now being sponged and pressed. Also, it has been reported to me that there were no flowers in the room occupied by the young lady with whom you were seen to arrive. This omission has now been rectified.

This kind of service went out with the war, never to return. Blix usually entrusted Haslev with his money, instructing the porter on no account to give him back more than his daily allowance, no matter what happened. Haslev and Blix had many an argument through the years over the allowance, but Haslev was firm and always won.

They don't make people like Blix anymore. The mould has been broken.

—POLLY PEABODY

I never heard him say anything bad about a soul—except Hitler.

—RUTH RASMUSSON

Nine

Polly and Mor: 1938–1946

N 1938, BLIX LEFT Kenya for good, suddenly, quietly, and finally. Winston Guest's family had leased Gardiner's Island outside New York City to develop as a wildfowl and sporting preserve. The bird life had been devastated by a hurricane some time before, and the Guests wanted Blix to restore the bird population and create a sporting area. He succeeded so well that at the first shoot, astonishing sport was shown and a record number of birds were brought down. The work on Gardiner's Island and the social whirl of New York was to be a very brief period of his life, for within a year it was clear that Europe was to be torn apart by war with Germany.

Then in the autumn of 1939, Russia suddenly invaded Finland. Blix, like all Swedes, was alarmed. He resigned from Gardiner's Island and with his friend, Count Folke Bernadotte, and the Finnish ambassador to the United States, set about raising money to create an American Field Hospital to go out to Finland. In no time, New York society was seized with a fervor to help "gallant Finland." Old atlases came out as smart New York matrons, uncertain of their geography, looked to see where exactly Finland was. Blix was the inspiration of the Aid for Finland scheme.

Polly Peabody, a young woman of twenty-two, had been turned down as an ambulance driver in France, as she was considered underage. Blix agreed to take her on as secretary to the American Field Hospital. By February 1940, they had raised over $100,000 and gathered up eight doctors, ten nurses, eighteen trucks, and loads of hospital supplies. Blix, through his powerful friends, had commandeered a Swedish vessel, the *SS Drottningholm,* and with forty-five tons of equipment on board, they sailed from New York on a wild March night, six months after the war had started in Europe.

The fact that Blix could awaken such a response is a tribute to the charm, enthusiasm, and leadership which he had shown in arranging safaris all through East and Central Africa. He was irresistible. At the time, there was a very strong isolationist movement in the United States. Like a protective moat, 3,000 miles of deep Atlantic waters separated the United States from Europe. Americans wished to remain insulated from conflict if at all possible. They did not want to be dragged into a European struggle, and anyone who suggested that Americans could be affected by it was to be shunned. Blix somehow overcame all opposition.

In 1986, Polly Peabody, looking back over forty years, wrote a letter to Romolus Kleen:

> I adored Blix. He was much older, so my admiration was limited by the age gap. He taught me to shoot and gave me a beautiful .2 bore gun which had belonged to the King of Sweden. This gun is still in the family. He told me so much about Kenya that when I went there fifteen years ago it was like coming home; I recognized it all. He had such a vivid touch and was a fascinating talker and teller of stories. There is no doubt Blix was a great leader. I think he could have got anyone to follow him anywhere. He had this wonderful vision, always taking the line that no task was impossible. And all this with that charming and endearing smile in the pale blue eyes.

Polly Peabody, with two uniformed field hospital colleagues and American journalist Arthur Menken.

Among their fellow travelers were twenty-eight wild Americans going to war. One of these, a black man from Harlem, claimed he was going to teach the Finns to fly. His record to date left one in doubt. Years before he had attempted a transatlantic flight from Harlem, but had taken the wrong direction and crashed, half a mile from home, in the Harlem flats. The laughing stock of his friends, he had then volunteered to fly for Haile Selassie, but soon wrapped the Emperor's plane around a tree. Finland was possibly his hope of another face-saving escape.

Apart from 1,500 chattering monkeys on their way to Finland for scientific purposes, there were also some wild Finns. Drinking fervently to the Finnish cause, they became more boisterous and daring as the nights progressed. Knife fights usually ensued. These entailed a competition as to how much of the pointed blade each competitor was able to endure. Anesthetized as they were, it was surprising none was killed. Closing their minds to these earthly beings were a group of nuns, who kept to themselves.

Two days out of Bergen Fjord, men were posted to look out for mines. The ship passed safely through and entered the fjord at dawn during the first week of April. By the time the ship had reached Norway, Blix had learned they were too late to be of any help to Finland: peace had been made between Finland and Russia in mid-March of 1940.

There were about twenty deserted freighters riding at anchor. It was later learned they were full of German soldiers awaiting orders to invade. Two days afterward, Bergen was overrun. For the moment, all was at peace. Delayed by orders to wait for the quays to be cleared, the ship was unable to dock for two hours, and the passengers missed the night train to Oslo. After unloading, equipment marked "FINLAND—HANDLE WITH CARE—THIS SIDE UP" lay strewn haphazardly over the quay. Standing awkwardly around it, in their unfamiliar gray uniforms and heavy boots, the American volunteers suddenly felt very alone, watching as their ship steamed out to sea.

The following morning Blix, Polly, and the medical staff caught the Oslo train, which failed to stop in Oslo: the German invasion had already begun. Mrs. Harriman, the United States minister, had organized a dinner party for them in Oslo, which they, of course, missed.

On April 8, Blix was once again back in Stockholm. There he learned Norway had been invaded. Rumors of a world war began to spread, and almost overnight Sweden started to mobilize. Shop windows were hastily boarded up as the Swedes waited their turn. Everyone talked in whispers and eyed one another with suspicion, for loyalties were divided.

When the field hospital equipment arrived in Stockholm, Blix made immediate plans to move it to Norway, which was now at war with Germany. Before leaving, he called on King Gustav at his summer palace just outside Stockholm to ask the aged king what Sweden's chances of entering the war were. The king told him that unless the country was invaded, Sweden would remain neutral. He then thanked Blix and his American friends for their efforts to support the Finnish cause.

With the news of the arrival of an Allied Expeditionary Force in Norway, Blix chose to move to Elverum, where the king of Norway had fled and been hunted down by German machine guns, and from there north to the south of Trondheim, where the fighting was taking place. At the Norwegian Frontier, Blix was told there was no hope of reaching the allies that way. Instead, he was to make for Namsos, where French and British forces were arriving in great numbers.

The following morning, the convoy bearing the American flag swung onto icy roads for the drive to Ostersund. There they were greeted by the townspeople, who clustered about the trucks, staring open-mouthed. They must have thought that American troops had entered the fight. In Ostersund, Blix met with the U.S. military attaché, who had just left Norway and was full of news. None of it was reassuring.

As the convoy rolled north toward the war zone, the country became more mountainous and snow laden, filled with endless forests of pine. The trucks were reloaded at Geddede, the last Swedish outpost, before entering Norway. Even there, it all seemed quiet and peaceful. It was not until the convoy moved slowly through the mountain passes that enemy planes were seen. These flew low overhead, without firing. Late that night, the convoy reached Grong. There the field hospital was to be housed in three buildings that, in prewar days, had been a women's college.

When the field hospital was set up, it contained two operating theaters and enough equipment to sustain a 200-bed capacity. It had been created to deal with hundreds of wounded, but the little enclave around Grong had so far produced no casualties, and the skilled staff had little to do.

The Norwegians are essentially peace-loving. They kept out of the Germans' way as much as possible, rather than have a confrontation. Walking down the road one morning, Blix was forced to duck as a German bomber swooped low overhead. When he asked a group of Norwegians nearby why they hadn't shot it down, they replied, "Oh, we couldn't do that. The Germans might shoot back at us."

In time, with the arrival of Allied troops, the little port of Namsos became a real target, taking a heavy beating, and the field hospital came into its own at last.

It did not last very long. The English and French soon abandoned Namsos, leaving one night under cover of darkness. It was rumored that the German advance was less than six hours away. As it was obvious they would not be allowed to stay, Blix decided to pull out. They were pursued by the Germans all the way to the Swedish border.

After the field hospital had returned to Sweden, Blix approached the French to offer it to them. The French were willing, but the State Department in Washington turned down the proposal. It seemed that the field hospital was destined to remain in abeyance. No one wished to make a decision.

Blix, too, was at a loss. He longed to play an active role in the war. Holland and Belgium had capitulated, and with Norway now at war, Sweden felt threatened on all sides. As a Swede, and a neutral, Blix was unable to join up. Polly Peabody wrote: "When I eventually arrived in England I tried to get Blix over. He was so keen to join the War and would have been an invaluable asset, but this was not to be."

Blix left Stockholm for the family seat at Nasbyholm, which now belonged to his nephew, Carl Frederik Blixen, and his young wife Manon. The young couple had given Blix the loan of a house on the estate.

Not unnaturally, the Swedes, finding themselves in the awkward position of being unable to fight and yet living in fear of invasion, continued to pursue their normal lives, heightened by intense moods and behavior. These were manifested in a social context: parties, race meetings, balls, hunts, and shoots were played out as though for the last time. With his reputation as one of Africa's finest shots, Blix was flooded with invitations.

In Sweden, as in many other European countries, it is necessary to crop the deer herds to maintain a natural balance between game and forestry.

The king, Gustav V, was present at such a shoot near Nasbyholm. Such was Blix's sporting reputation in Sweden that the king insisted that he be given the position of honor. Probably put off his stride by this royal patronage, Blix missed a magnificent, standing red deer—not once but three times. The other guns, amused, were beginning to wonder if all they'd heard was true. Then, three more deer ran out at full speed. Blix fired three shots in quick succession; all three deer rolled over like rabbits.

That evening, as the men warmed themselves in front of the fire, animated by large glasses of brandy, the talk of sporting feats became more and more vivid, and more and more imaginative. The Duke d'Otrante sat apart from his friends, looking disapproving. In a moment's lull in the conversation, a loud exclamation of disbelief could be heard from his corner of the room. "D'Otrante! You miserable immigrant," laughed Blix. "Do you consider yourself too good for the Swedish nobility?"

Everyone laughed, for d'Otrante was indeed rather pompous.

Inquired the king from the next room, "Have I missed something, d'Otrante?"

D'Otrante stood up and, with a slight inclination of his

Blix and his brother's son, Carl-Frederik.

head, replied, "Nothing that is worth repeating, Your Majesty." And he quietly left the room.

During these last years in Sweden, Blix saw a lot of his nephew and Manon, Carl-Fredrik's pretty young wife. She doted on him and saw that he was as much part of the life at Nasbyholm as possible. At a christening party for their first-born son, a lot of old friends were gathered. At the midnight supper the table groaned under an abundance of little dishes:

smoked reindeer, herrings marinated in every conceivable way, smoked eel, meatballs, smoked salmon, eggs, and fish roe. To wash it all down were rows of chilled aquavit. Traditionally, on such occasions, each glass downed is accompanied by a song. As they were to begin, Manon realized Blix was absent. Guttural voices led her to the library, where she found Blix intently teaching the priest a bawdy song in German, a language with which the poor priest was unfamiliar.

Gustav Wrangel, Blix's childhood friend, came to stay. Gustaf wanted to see the house at Stjerneholm where Blix had lived when he managed the farm as a young man, so Blix made a day of it. They collected Manon and Carl-Frederik, who wanted to see the well in which Blix was known to have stored his aquavit. Aquavit must be considered the national drink of Sweden; it should always be served chilled, preferably encased in ice. Blix would lower the bottles on a string into the well, where they soon attained the required temperatures. (A couple of years ago, the well ran dry and the present owner of Nasbyholm, Dick Blixen, hired two men to make it deeper. Checking their progress later in the day, he found the two men lolling drunkenly under a tree, very much the worse for wear. Their undoing had been two of Blix's aquavit bottles, discovered still at the bottom of the well.)

The young farm manager, Hans Nilsson, was surprised by the visit, but he was happy to show them around. He offered them coffee, inevitably laced with brandy, and when he saw how much they were all enjoying themselves, he invited them to stay on for lunch. The lunch, washed down with aquavit, was followed by more brandy, until the young man's cellar was finally depleted. On the way home Blix remarked, "What a party we gave Nilsson today. He must be so happy."

The Swedes, and all Scandinavians for that matter, have a reputation for hard drinking. Perhaps it is their cold, north-

ern climate. Blix was a true example of his nation, but he rarely attained a condition of intoxication. Leaving Gustaf Wrangel's estate, Ellinge, to catch a train after a particularly good lunch, he noticed, as he was about to board, a sign: INTOXICATED PERSONS ARE PROHIBITED FROM TRAVELING ON THIS TRAIN. With due regard for the law, Blix returned to Ellinge.

The following morning, he woke up early for a stroll round the grounds. As he returned to the house, his hostess met him at the door and asked if he was thirsty. "Yes, as a matter of fact I am." She handed him a glass of water. Blix looked at it disapprovingly and said, "I did say thirsty, not dirty."

The summer months were spent happily at Falsterbo, a resort in the south of Sweden. Those that could afford it had houses there, congregating at Falsterbo's fashionable hotel on the beach. I was then a very small boy and spent my days on the beach and in the water, stark naked. Blix, who was staying with us, one day suggested that refreshments were called for, and he and I proceeded to the rather elegant bar at the hotel. Here he planted me, still completely naked, on one of the bar-stools, and I carefully repeated what, on the way up, he had told me to say: "One large gin and tonic for my friend, one lemonade for me, and charge the lot to my father."

It was in Falsterbo that Blix met Ruth. Recalling Blix's advice to Romolus, Ruth was a woman with a business of her own. She ran a successful kennel and bred Riessen-

(Preceding page) *A delightful picture of love and happiness. Lilla Mor's and Blix's life together was very harmonious, and they were never bored with each other. She understood him better than any of his previous women and she was exactly what he needed.*

Ruth and Bror at Nasbyholm, 1943

schnauzers. She was certainly independent, a quality that all Blix's women shared. Unlike the others, Ruth had reached that stage in life when a calmer, more detached reckoning had replaced youthful passions. She was practical and down-to-earth, but not dour. Blix came to love her and called her affectionately "Lilla Mor," my little mother. Lilla Mor was eventually shortened to Mor, which was the name everyone came to know her by.

Mor had a house on the coast, not far from Nasbyholm, where Blix joined her. There, he wrote his second book, *Letters from Africa*. The book was published in Swedish and, sadly, not translated. It was a much better book than *Nyama,* written in a quieter, more settled frame of mind.

Blix, too, was older, his violent passions spent. In Mor, he found easy companionship and a loyal friend. She was not in the least bit jealous of his friends, and never interfered. His absences were never questioned. She was his rock, someone to whom he could always return to laugh with over his escapades and wayward wanderings. She told me:

> Why should I not share this wonderful man? He was always so kind and considerate to me. Generous to a fault. In the war I was a heavy smoker and, as you know, tobacco was severely rationed. Blix always gave me his coupons. It wasn't until years later that I learned he loved cigars. We had so much fun together. They were the happiest years of my life. When Blix died, I never met a man to match him.

Those war years were lived to the full. The seasons turned; peace was declared. Blix felt that perhaps he should return to Gardiner's Island to continue the work he had started there. Somehow, the will was lacking. Sweden was his home, and to his home, like the prodigal son, he had finally returned.

On May 3, 1946, Corfitz Beck-Friis was due to collect Blix and Mor to take them to Borringekloster, his home, from where they were to go on to a party. Blix looked out of

A gentleman has discreetly removed his shoes, his hat, and his monocle to cool off on the beach. A generation is gone, never to return.

the window at the flurries of snow falling while waiting for Corfitz to arrive. He heard the car brake to a stop outside the door and picked up their suitcases just as Mor, adjusting her scarf, arrived at the bottom of the stairs.

"Come on, you two. We're off," said Corfitz, as he held the door open for Mor. Blix climbed in back. "We have plenty of time to get changed at my place. Tonight's will be the best party ever!" The three friends were in a happy mood as they approached Corfitz's home.

The drive to Borringekloster is lined with a long avenue of lime trees, now stark and rigid in winter's grip. The icy surface of the drive made for tricky driving, and for a second Corfitz lost control. Blix threw his arms around Mor to stop her going into the windshield. The car hit a tree. Blix was killed.

The man whom women loved was no more.

A great sadness spread over the whole country. Blix was mourned by thousands. For many months trackers, gunbearers, skinners, and all his other friends wandered about with drooping faces and dim eyes. Another great man had gone to the Happy Hunting Grounds.

—KRISTER ASCHAN

Index

G

H

J

K

L

M

N

O

P

R

S

T

U

V

W